The Sky Is Not The Limit,
YOU ARE!

By Bob Davies

ISBN 1-881461-06-8

Published by In-Fact Publishing Co., Carlsbad, California

For Ordering Information, Contact:
High Performance Training
5431 Sierra Verde
Irvine, California 92715

To: Bob Davies
From: Mike Grumet

Dear Bob:

I want to thank you for providing me with the training that
has greatly enhanced my performance. About 3 years ago I
went to your all-day seminar in Anaheim. I learned several
lessons and insights from that program:

1. How to be accountable for my activities.
2. How to measure my performance.
3. How to set realistic goals on a (weekly) basis.
4. How to overcome fear.
5. How to organize my life in a meaningful way.

The results of the seminar are as follows:

1. While I was in advertising, I overcame fear of approach-
ing new industries not represented in my magazine. During my
final quarter of sales with that company, I set records,
most of it from an industry other reps would not touch.

2. Now, I overcame the fear of giving up 13 years of client
base and a substantial income for an opportunity to help
people in a new career of financial services. I am taking
slow and steady steps to build a lifelong clientele. In the
meantime, as a result of early success with the business
community, the company has hired me an assistant to book appointments for my special business niche.

I am confident with the training techniques provided by you,
that I will double or triple my income from my previous career within 3 years. When I do, please invite me to one of
your seminars to speak about the success of your program.

Last, I want to tell you in addition to my career development I am a much happier and active person. I sit on 2 fund-
raising boards, the YMCA board for Indian Guides and help on
committees of all types, etc. In addition, I still make time
for my family and friends. All in all, I have found time and
energy to be a better PARTICIPANT in life vs. an OBSERVER.

Thanks again,

Mike Grumet
New York Life Insurance Company
Brea, California

TABLE OF CONTENTS

Introduction

Several years ago, according to a story I heard, a couple flew home to California from the East Coast on a major commercial airline. They checked their luggage curbside. Included was a dog in an animal carrier.

After an uneventful, even pleasant, flight they went to the baggage claim area. After a short wait, the luggage started to tumble down the belt onto the circling conveyer. Finally, their familiar bags appeared one by one—all except the dog in the special cage.

Before panic set in, they realized that perhaps the cage was an oversized item and would be delivered to a different area. After getting directions, they went to that area. No dog.

Well, off it was to the baggage claim office to show their baggage tags and fill out a lost-luggage form. A courteous attendant told them not to worry. The dog was probably on the next flight. Airline personnel would deliver the dog to their home as soon as it showed up.

"Don't worry," he said. "Go home and get some rest. We'll take care of your dog."

They took his advice and went home.

Now the airline baggage handlers at the terminal went to work searching for the lost dog. They couldn't find it anywhere in the usual places it might be. Perhaps it really was on another flight or routed to the wrong destination in error.

One of the handlers suddenly noticed what looked like

an animal carrier behind some crates. Sure enough, the claim-ticket numbers matched. It was the lost dog. There was one small problem: The dog was dead.

With panic and embarrassment a group of people gathered around the dead dog. What were they going to do?

Someone suggested, "Why don't we buy a dog just like that one?"

Everyone thought that was a great idea. With cage in hand, one of the handlers went out in search of a look-alike, stand-in dog.

He found one that was a perfect match, put it into the animal carrier, and went off to deliver it.

When the couple answered the door, the handler proudly said, "Here's your dog!"

The man heard the dog whimpering inside the carrier and said, "That's not my dog!"

The handler asked, "How do you know it's not your dog? You didn't even look inside."

The man responded, "Because my dog's dead. We were bringing it home to bury it."

Whether this is a true story or not, the message is clear: Be honest.

That is exactly what I am going to do in this book. I will be brutally honest with you. When you are finished with this book you will be armed with no-nonsense performance tools that will create leverage stronger than anything you have ever experienced.

The techniques I am going to share with you are life changing. I know from experience that they work, and thousands of people who have attended my workshops in almost every state in the United States, every province in Canada, and in Australia know they work.

Our work is cut out for us because of our fears, circumstances, priorities, interruptions, excuses, and reasons. The good news is: If you have made a decision for improvement, these techniques will work *immediately*.

You and I will explore the crisis of fear., then move into the sources of empowerment that are available to us. You will actually learn a systematic approach to *focus* through strategic planning and *accountability* through the outstanding technique of partnering. You will learn how to reinforce these techniques so that results are long term. You will learn how to turn intentions into actual performance.

Chapter 1
The Crisis of Fear

It's an unreasoning terror, an irrational panic that clutches at your throat and offers no avenue of escape; a fear that alerts you to no real danger, yet it causes the heart to pound, the blood pressure to rise, and the palms to sweat. When it strikes, your pupils will dilate, your hair will bristle, your muscles will tense up. It will be difficult to swallow, and you may be nauseated and feel that you are about to faint. Most of all, you will want to run to escape, to avoid.

Phobias—unreasoning fears—are not new. They are a part of human nature. The ancient Greeks had a general fear of illness. They often painted the likeness of one of their gods related to health on their battle shields. The idea was to spread the fear of illness to the enemy.

Two thousand years ago, Hippocrates described a man who was frightened each time he heard the sound of a flute. France's King Henry III refused to have anything to do with cats. Augustus Caesar refused to sit in the dark. A French playwright refused to go out into the dark.

Even Sigmund Freud couldn't work his way out of a phobia. He was reported to be afraid of traveling on a train. Howard Hughes feared germs. Alfred Hitchcock feared police. Any number of well-known celebrities refuse to take to the skies for fear of flying.

Nineteen million Americans have a strong phobia of

some type or another, and *millions more have intense fears of the activities they want to do to reach their goals!*

What is this thing called fear?

Some time ago I was in Chicago for a program and I was staying in a 54-story building. I went up to the sun deck for some reason. When I got there, I went to the edge and leaned over the railing. The railing was up to my chest, and I was completely safe, yet I felt the sudden grip of fear. My conscious, rational mind knew that nothing bad could happen to me, but my subconscious mind still caused my body to tense up. I decided that some day I would confront this fear. *Some day,* I would jump out of an airplane. *Some day.*

Several months passed. One Saturday morning I was watching a television program about a group of Japanese sky divers who had traveled to the United States for special instruction at Perris, Calif. I decided to go to Perris and confront my fear of heights and do a skydive.

When I arrived the first thing I saw was a sign:

> WARNING
> SKYDIVING IS A HIGH-RISK
> ACTIVITY THAT MAY RESULT IN
> INJURY AND DEATH

I was already feeling uneasy. Seeing that sign didn't relax me any.

It got worse. They have you fill out a waiver waiving your right (or anyone else's right) to sue if you are injured or killed. Then they show you a video of someone telling you that this is a dangerous sport and that the waiver has held up in court.

It got even worse! All the training was about what could happen that would kill you.

What would you do if you can't find your rip cord? I said,

"You find it." They said, "Good answer. How long do you look for it?" I said, "Until you find it." They said "No. If you do that you will bounce." (That is their term for hitting the ground before your parachute opens.) "You reach for it twice, then you pull your reserve."

What happens if you pull your main parachute and you look up and there are lines over the canopy? The answer is: You do a "canopy control check" and see if you can fly the canopy. If you can't, you pull a yellow cut-away handle that releases the main parachute and free-fall again. When you are stable, you open your reserve parachute.

All of this talk about all the things that could go wrong made me exhausted with nervous energy.

Finally the training was over. While waiting for the instructor to bring my parachute, I glanced down and saw a copy of a magazine called *Parachutist*. I opened it and there was a page headed "Incident Reports." It was a list of the people who had died the month before while sky diving, and why. The categories: number of jumps (usually one!), cause of death (always impact).

My instructor brought my parachute and laid it at my feet. He pointed at it. "See this small pin? This will save your life." He left me with this unfamiliar life-saving equipment to get an altimeter. I looked down and saw a label that read: "WARNING: TRAINING AND OR EXPERIENCE ARE REQUIRED TO REDUCE THE RISK OF INJURY, HARD OPENINGS OR DEATH. YOU MUST HAVE AT LEAST 100 RAM AIR JUMPS TO USE THIS EQUIPMENT".

I wondered, "Is this the right gear for me? What do you have to do to survive in this sport?"

I kept thinking of what my secretary said to me when I told her I was going to jump out of an airplane: "I have a bad feeling about this. Would you sign my check before you go?" I could only hope she wasn't a psychic!

Finally my instructor said it was time to go to the plane. I said, "Any word from the governor?" He didn't answer.

The plane is a twin Otter called "Jaws." When we're all aboard, I notice I'm the only student in a plane load of sky divers.

As the plane takes off and climbs, my conscious mind is telling me, "This is safe.You are well trained at the most successful and largest drop zone in the world. Your jump masters have made thousands of jumps. They know what they're doing. You have two parachutes. Main parachutes open without problems 99% of the time. If it doesn't, you have a professionally packed reserve parachute."

My subconscious mind is telling me, "*You're going to die!*"

Finally, the plane is at 12,500 feet. One of the experienced skydivers opens the door and sticks his head out to "spot" the airplane. They are kneeling in the door, looking for a mark on the ground that indicates we are over the target landing area. When we are, they tell the pilots to cut back on the power to the engines, reducing forward airspeed. Then a group climbs out of the door and jumps out, immediately disappearing.

Three groups leave, then it's my turn. I carefully inched my way to the door. I felt my legs go almost numb as I positioned myself in the door. I gave the command "Ready, set go!" and jumped out with my jump masters on each side of me.

At 5,000 feet, as I was supposed to, I signaled and pulled my rip cord. To my complete delight I saw a perfectly beautiful canopy, except for a "line twist," open over my head. I'd been told what to do about a line twist and did it.

I looked for the drop zone and did a stand-up landing.

As I was driving home, the adrenaline was still pumping through my body. I looked up at the clouds with a new appreciation. The sky would never be the same for me. The sky was now recreation. This transformation is called creating a new paradigm, a new perception.

But I wasn't completely cured of my fear, and I wanted to get rid of it. I took a course called "Accelerated Free Fall," which consisted of about eight jumps with a progression of skill. Each of those jumps was horrible for me. I was in a state of fear-induced panic. It felt so good to land, get in my car, and drive home. But that bothered me. I wanted to beat this fear. I remember seeing an experienced jump master eating a sandwich on the plane en route to altitude. I kept thinking, "How could he possibly do that?" My stomach was in my throat.

I finally finished all my student training and could jump by myself or with a group without any supervision. I was absolutely terrified for my first 20 jumps. Sometime after that I finally started to feel comfortable in the door of an airplane and jumping out

I had arrived! I could now do an activity that at first terrified me. It was the same activity, but through repetition and being persistent I conquered the fear. I've now made more than 1,000 jumps, and skydiving is one of the most peaceful activities I do.

> **FEAR IS AN ILLUSION! FEAR IS A LIE!**
> **When you confront the fear and embrace the fear,**
> **you erase the fear!**

My sky diving experience may seem an extreme example of our fears and how we can overcome them, but all fear is the same, whether it is fear of big things or of small things.

Fear is fear, and it is what prevents us from doing even the things we tell ourselves we *want* to do.

For example, I had a long-standing problem with my weight. I knew what to do, and I wanted to do it. But I was absolutely terrified of the possibility of being hungry. Because of that fear, I thought I couldn't lose weight. I've always exercised, but I ate too much. In time, by conquering the fear of being hungry, *by using the system I'm going to reveal to you*, I broke through the attitude that I couldn't do it. I lost the weight I wanted to lose and I've maintained the weight I want to have.

In the same way, I broke the habit of biting my nails. During one period of my life, I would bite my nails until they bled. Again, *using the system I'm going to reveal to you*, I broke through the fear that led me to nail biting.

Today, I comfortably handle the situations that used to produce fear inside me. The situations haven't changed. The external circumstances that produced the fear that produced the behavior have not changed.

What did change? By *using the system I'm going to reveal to you*, my paradigm changed. My perception of the circumstances changed. This system helps you change perceptions in such a way that you do what you have decided you would commit to doing. The principles in this book will enable you to leverage yourself and defeat fear.

In the meantime, try the following the next time you have fear:

1. Rate your anxiety on a 1 to 10 scale;
2. Expect and allow the fear to arise and accept that you have a fear;
3. When fear appears, wait and let it be;
4. Focus on and do a manageable activity, such as deep breathing, in the present;
5. Function with a level of fear and appreciate your accomplishment; and
6. Expect and allow the fear to reappear.

Think about this in terms of asking someone out on a date,

or of standing up to your boss, or in making a prospecting cold call.

> **FEAR, REGARDLESS OF THE CIRCUMSTANCE, IS THE SAME ENTITY AND CREATES THE SAME PHYSIOLOGY**

Chapter 2
The Problem:
Human Nature Does Not Support
High Achievement

Human nature does not support high achievement! The first principle of human nature related to achievement is:

THINK ⟶ FEEL ⟶ ACT

**THE WAY YOU THINK
AFFECTS THE WAY YOU FEEL**

**THE WAY YOU FEEL
DETERMINES WHAT YOU WILL DO**

Put another way: Your thoughts affect your physiology, and that affects the choices you make and the actions you take.

Let me say it a third way: You are not going to do what you don't feel like doing.

For example, you may be very interested in losing weight. On a Sunday, you go to a weight control seminar, you set specific goals. You are motivated. On Monday, however, if you don't *feel* like getting up at 5 a.m. and going to the gym to exercise, you are not going to do it.

If you don't *feel* like going into the office in the evening and making prospecting calls, you are not going to do it. If you don't *feel* like cleaning your desk or spending time with your family and friends, you are not going to do it no matter how committed to balance you say you are.

Our first human resistance is that we are not going to do what we don't feel like doing consistently.

You might have firm intentions, you might be motivated, but if you don't feel like doing what has to be done to reach a goal, you're not going to do it. We can illustrate this with an iceberg (Figure 1).

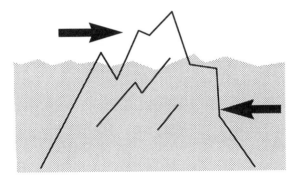

Figure 1

The arrow from the left is the wind. The arrow from the right is the current. In which direction will the iceberg float? It will float in the direction of the current because most of its mass is being affected by the current. Even if there were a hurricane at the surface, the iceberg would still go along with the current.

The tip of the iceberg represents your intentions, or your conscious mind. The submerged mass represents your "support system," your subconscious mind: the way you think (Figure 2).

This concept of thought affecting action is not pop psychology. It is grounded in scientific research. Scientists have conducted research proving that your thoughts affect your physiological processes, and these physiological processes, linked to your automatic survival mechanism,

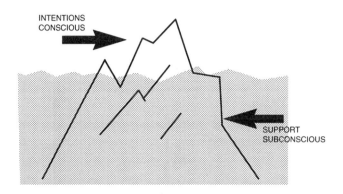

Figure 2

dictate what you are going to do no matter what you consciously tell yourself you want to do.

Research has shown that your thoughts affect your physical body. When you don't *feel* like doing something you *tell yourself* you want to do, you set up a physiological chain reaction that creates stress.Every thought is a physiological reaction in your body. A thought is created by an impulse response resulting in an exchange of chemicals, as illustrated in Figure 3.

When you have a thought you are creating a *reality* now! A thought is a physical reality in the present. We create our reality through our imagination.

According to physicists, all matter is composed of energy. The surface of a table, for example, seems solid, but it is really composed of molecules that are "glued" together by energy fields. In turn, these molecules are composed of atoms that are also held together by energy fields. And inside these atoms are even smaller particles that stay in one another's vicinity because of their electrical (energy) attraction to one another. If all this energy attraction were to disappear suddenly, the tabletop would dissipate in front of your eyes and no longer exist as a tabletop.

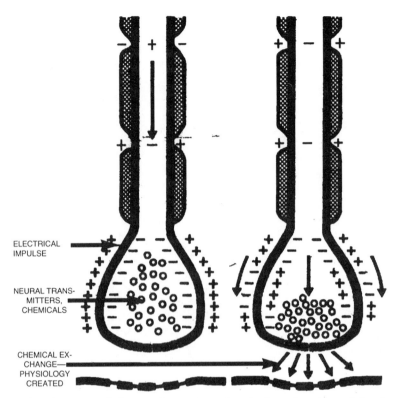

A thought is created when an electrical impulse stimulates the release of chemicals. These chemicals are real physiological states. Your thoughts create internal realities even before the actual external accomplishment. You are what you think!

Figure 3

We are like that tabletop in that our fundamental composition is also basically energy. Everything that goes on inside our bodies, including our thoughts, is caused by the interplay of energy and in turn causes other energy interplays.

In fact, the energy in our bodies is so powerful, it extends beyond us! Scientists in this century have proved that there is such a thing as the human "aura," a field of energy that extends out from our bodies for 50 feet in all directions and 12 feet into the ground. They can even photograph the human aura by using what is known as Kirlian photography.

Kirlian was a researcher in the U.S.S.R. in the early 20th century. One day he was demonstrating the process to some high-placed officials in the Soviet scientific fraternity. To his dismay, it wasn't working. When he photographed his hand, the aura didn't come out right. It was dull, gray, barely distinct.

He disassembled the apparatus, checked it, and reassembled it. It still didn't work right. Just about then, he became ill and went off to bed. His wife, who had assisted him in his research, begged the scientific big-wigs to give her the chance to prove the machine worked. She carried on the demonstration, and it did work! Her hand showed a healthy, strong aura.

Her husband had been so worried about the demonstration he became ill, which altered his aura, which made him even more worried, which made him even more ill. His wife didn't have the same level of anxiety, so she was able to carry on the demonstration and show a healthy, strong aura.

Here, Kirlian proved our premise: What you think affects the way you feel, which affects the way you act. His thinking was negative, which made him feel ill, which made him give up.

We are energy systems that constantly radiate energy. A researcher at Yale, for example, asserts from his research that all living things are surrounded by and connected by a web of measurable dynamic energy fields; that there is an exchange of energy going on inside us and between us and our environment.

Did you ever have a strong first impression about someone, either positive or negative? According to research, this happens when your aura interacts with that person's aura. If the auras are in harmony, you will have an instantly positive impression of the person.

Our cells are energy systems. We are energy systems. We are constantly interacting with the energy systems of other people. There's a dance that goes on. Language is only one form of communication. We also communicate through brain waves and sound waves, through different types of energy waves in the environment.

The brain energy of one person can impose its rhythm onto the brain energy of another. This is called spontaneous telepathy.

Proof of this concept of thought transference was given in a paper by Cleve Baxter, "Evidence of Primary Perception in Plant Life," published in the 1968 *International Journal of Parapsychology*.

Baxter was a lie-detector expert. He hooked plants up to a lie detector and directed thoughts at them. In one experiment, he thought about burning the plants. The lie-detector graphs showed that when he left the room to get a match, the electromagnetic activity in the plants surged. It was the same pattern human beings make when they are frightened. If the plants had had legs, they would have run away!

In another experiment, Baxter dumped some living brine shrimp into a cup of boiling water. At the moment of impact, when the shrimp died, there was another surge of electromagnetic energy among the plants. Somehow, the plants "knew"the shrimp were being killed. There was some sort of telepathic communication happening.

We don't have to conduct laboratory experiments with electrodes and matches and brine shrimp and boiling water to have proof of this spontaneous telepathy. It's proven every season in the world of sports.

The 1993 baseball season in the United States is a prime example. Here is an analysis of the National League's home games for that season:

	Home Games			Away Games		
	Won	Lost	% Won	Won	Lost	% Won
Philadelphia	52	29	64	45	36	55
Montreal	55	26	67	39	42	48
St. Louis	49	32	60	38	43	46
Chicago	43	38	53	41	40	50
Pittsburgh	40	41	49	35	46	43
Florida	35	46	43	25	56	30
New York	28	53	34	31	50	38
Atlanta	51	30	62	53	28	65
San Francisco	50	31	61	53	28	65
Houston	44	37	54	41	40	50
Los Angeles	41	40	50	40	41	49
Cincinnati	41	40	50	32	49	39
Colorado	39	42	48	28	53	34
San Diego	34	47	41	27	54	33

There is something going on here! In only three cases did a team win a greater percentage of away games than of home games. Is it any wonder the season's games are split evenly between home and away? The spontaneous telepathy of the crowd at home—positive, winning thoughts—gave the teams heightened performance. You might say, "Of course the teams do better. They can hear the crowd yelling approval."

What about the telepathy between mother and child when they aren't in the same room, and can't hear one another? There are hundreds of recorded examples of this type of telepathy. In a clinic where the mothers are in a different section, separate from their babies, they can't possibly hear them, yet a mother will exhibit nervousness when her baby cries.

Taking this even further, another researcher conducted an experiment with a mother rabbit and her babies. He put the litter in a submarine that went deep below the surface of the ocean. He implanted electrodes in the brain of the mother, which was kept in the laboratory on land. The mother rabbit could have no direct experience of what happened to her young. Yet, when his assistants aboard the submarine killed the litter one by one, the mother rabbit's brain registered anxiety at the same time each of the young died.

There can be no doubt that our thoughts are much more powerful than we've ever known, and that we are in constant non-verbal communication with our environment and other people—even when we don't see them.

Our thoughts, our aura of energy, can even move objects. This is called telekinesis, and it has been proven a fact in laboratory studies.

The Russians made a thorough study of one woman who was known to have this telekinetic energy. They hooked her up to various instruments to record heart rate, respiration, brain waves, electromagnetic field, and the like. She sat at a table and moved her hands above some objects on the table. The EEG showed tremendous activity in the regions of the brain related to sight. Her heart rate increased to 240 beats a minute. The objects on the table began to move. As they did so, her electromagnetic field, her aura, began to pulse. Her brain waves and heart rate pulsed in harmony with the energy pulse. It was as though her entire being was sending a wave of energy to the objects, making them move.

Here is a classic example of mind over matter; or, more correctly, of mind energy over matter energy.

All of this research has given us a new picture of the human being. We are not alienated creatures apart from nature. We are integral parts of nature enmeshed in a web of energy that flows and ebbs throughout all of Creation.

In my seminars, I demonstrate this concept of how our own thoughts and the thoughts of others affect us by using a simple muscle test. I have a participant come up on the stage and have him hold an arm out parallel to the floor, straight out from the side at shoulder height. I ask him to strenuously resist when I try to push his arm down. That gives us a "control" resistance to measure what happens next.

I ask him to close his eyes and think a positive thought and resist while I try to push his arm down. The resistance is usually very firm. Then I ask him to think a negative thought. The resistance is significantly weaker.

Then I ask him to leave the room. When he is gone, I tell the audience that I am going to continue the experiment using their thoughts. I tell them that after the subject returns to the room, I am going to once again ask him to close his eyes and hold his arm out. When I hold up one finger, I want the rest of the participants to think negative thoughts. When I hold up two fingers; positive thoughts.

You can probably guess what happens. When the audience thinks negative thoughts, the subject's resistance is noticeably weak. When the audience thinks positive thoughts, the subject's resistance is notably stronger.

This is yet one more experiment that gives credibility to our equation:

$$\text{THINK} \longrightarrow \text{FEEL} \longrightarrow \text{ACT}$$

But just how does thought affect how we feel?

Every thought we have creates a chemical exchange in the brain. The most interesting thing is that different types of thought create different types of reactions in different parts of the brain!

Experiments have shown that a positive thought, whether from yourself or others, stimulates the part of your brain called the septum. The septum controls the thalamus, which secretes endorphins. Endorphins give the organism a feeling of well-being, of peace and euphoria. If you think about great things happening to you, about pleasure, about love, the septum is going to tell the thalamus to release a good dose of endorphins. You will have a powerful, healthy state of mind.

If, however, you were to start thinking of deals falling apart, of rejection, of people who have let you down, of disappointment, the electrical energy in your brain will be centered in the amygdala. The receptor sites for endorphins are shut down. The endorphins in your system cannot be absorbed. Further, the production of endorphins is stopped. You are going to feel awful (Figure 4).

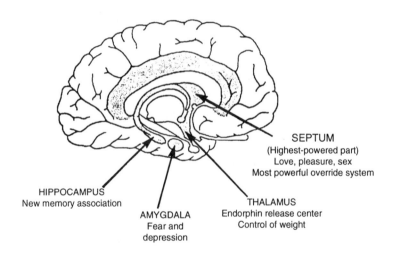

Figure 4

All of this proves one important point: To be high achievers, we have to control our thoughts. Our thoughts have to be positive so our endorphin supply stays high.

Most people agree with my first point about human nature, that human nature does not support high achievement. To counteract that, many people, companies, and organizations have for the past 10 years or so turned to goal setting.

Remember the story about the lost, dead dog replaced by a look-alike, live dog. I'm going to be brutally honest and say something that goes against what you have heard for years:

**GOAL SETTING BY ITSELF
DOES NOT WORK!**

Don't misunderstand. I do advocate goal setting, but not by itself. Goal setting by itself is an incomplete process. If all you do is set goals, you will be very disappointed. Have you ever said you would do something and you were motivated to do it, and then you didn't accomplish it? Have you ever said you were going to lose 10 pounds and you intended to exercise and diet, and at the end of the month you found you had *gained* five pounds? What happened?

Look at Figure 5. On the top line is the word *intentions*. This is what you intend to do, your goals and activities. There is another word that goes there. I just cringe when I hear it. The word is *potential*. The reason I cringe is that your potential is not relevant. What you are capable of doing does not pay your mortgage. It is only the bottom line that counts—not what you *say* you are going to do, but

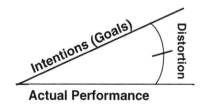

Figure 5

what you actually get accomplished. You do not get paid for trying or working hard. You get paid for *results*.

Here's an example. I was doing my program for a mortgage company in San Diego in 1986. This was a single-family residential resale lending company working with primarily one to four units and some builder business. The interest rate in 1982 had been 16.02%. By 1986 it had fallen to 8.5%.

The company put an ad in the newspaper offering refinancing loans and the phone was ringing off the hook. They were getting more calls because of that ad than they had from any ad before. The loan reps, who were commission-only salespeople, were coming into the office, sitting at their desks, and answering the calls. They were doing more business than ever.

They had a wise manager who recognized a trend and called a meeting. In this meeting he said they needed to realize they lived in a cyclical marketplace and that the interest rates would change. They had to keep a balance between the refinancing loans and the resale loans made through real estate agents. They had to continue to call on their real estate agents to keep the momentum going in that area. In short, they had to get out into the field and prospect.

The loan reps all agreed, and said that each would talk to 20 new people that week who could give them business. They committed to 20 new contacts. They *wanted* to make 20 new contacts, they were *motivated*, they *recognized the need* to do so, and they *intended* to contact 20 new people.

They *said* they would, they *wanted* to. *They did not do it!*

When they were asked why they didn't make the 20 new contacts they said they would make, the response was, "I was going to, but I was just . . .

TOO BUSY!

We all have perceptions and filters from which and through which we see the world. "Too busy" is just a perception. It's a point of view, or a paradigm, as was my fear of heights. Why did the loan reps think they were too busy? Lets look at the world as they saw it through their filters:

- I was all set to prospect, but my manager came up to me and said that one of the properties I have a loan on had a crack in the driveway and in the foundation, and I needed to get a geology report today or that loan would not be submitted for funding. I get paid when this loan funds, so it was a priority that I take care of this. I can't worry about the possibility of new business when I have a problem with existing business. I'll get to the prospecting as soon as I take care of this.

- I was all set to prospect, then my processor came up to me and told me that this other loan was a buy-down. The borrower was moving from a three-bedroom, two-bath home in a beautiful area to a two-bedroom, one-bath in an older, beat-up area, and I had to verify that it was going to be owner occupied. I will get to the prospecting as soon as I handle this.

- My processor comes up to me and tells me that she made a mistake on loan-to-value on another loan—it's not 52%, it's 82%. That puts the loan into mortgage insurance and I have to contact the borrower and tell them their payments are going to be higher than expected. I'll get to the prospecting soon. I really will.

- Underwriting wants bank statements on this other loan as well as verification of rental income. The bank statements will show declining income. I'll have to get with my manager on this right away.

- An appraisal comes in too low on this other property and the borrower wants to renege on the deal on this other loan. I have to see if I can salvage this one.

- There is a ding on this other borrower's credit and I need a letter from Sears today.

- I have out-of-town family coming in today and I have to get to the airport to pick them up right now.

In short: "I was going to prospect, but I was just too busy!"

Look at the line in Figure 6. Is the line concave or convex? It's both. Whether you see it as concave or convex depends on your viewpoint.

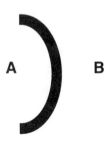

Figure 6

If you were facing this line from Point A, you would say it's concave. From Point B, it looks convex.

Now, at Point A, you will gather "evidence" to support your point of view that the line is concave. Once you have that evidence, your brain will put up strong resistance to any change in your point of view (Figure 7). Resistance follows evidence.

Figure 7

If you were to try to go through that line, to where it would look convex, you would be stopped by the resistance caused by the "evidence" your brain has so conveniently concocted for you.

The person at Point B has the same problem. The person at Point B has gathered all sorts of evidence that the line is convex, and that person will strongly resist any suggestion that it could also be concave.

The truth about this line is that it is both concave and convex. The only difference is point of view.

> YOU MUST LEVERAGE YOURSELF TO
> SELECT THE POINT OF VIEW THAT
> SUPPORTS HIGH ACHIEVEMENT

Point of view—perception—affects the way you think, which in turn affects the way you feel, which in turn affects what you do.

Some time ago, I was doing a series of programs in New Jersey. I was staying at my mother's house, where my sister and her three small children were also living.

One morning I rose early, about 5 a.m., to get ready for a

program. I went to the refrigerator, looking for a light breakfast. There was a bottle of orange juice on the shelf. I took it out and shook it. The top was loose, and orange juice went everywhere: on the floor, on me.

Now, there are two possible perceptions I could have of this event. I can either take responsibility for what happened or I can be a victim and not take responsibility for what happened.

If I decide to be the victim, I'd be thinking, "Why doesn't my sister teach her kids to put the cap on tight when they put something into the refrigerator?"

If I decide to take responsibility, I'd be thinking, "I'd better make sure the cap is tight before I shake a bottle of orange juice."

A minor incident you say? Not even worth thinking about? Let's take a look at another incident—one that cost me $10,000.

I was investing in property with some people who had created a no-money-down system. The man in charge of the operation was named Michael. The idea was that I'd give them $10,000 and 30 days later they'd give me a check for $11,000.

The first deal worked out fine. I got my money back, with interest, as promised. The next time, I gave Michael a check for $10,000. He was a week past the 30 days in paying me this time, but he tossed an extra $100 on top to make up for it.

The next time, Michael suggested I write the investment check out to him, personally. He didn't have the paperwork ready, but said he'd get it to me later. He was in a hurry because the deal was sweet and almost ready to go into escrow.

Thirty days passed and Michael had not yet repaid me. I was a little concerned, but then I got a check in the mail for $11,000. I was mystified because the check was drawn on the account of a woman I didn't know, but I deposited the check and forgot about it. Until it bounced.

I called the person who had introduced me to Michael and found that Michael had done the same thing to him. I called the police. They knew of him. I called the woman whose name was on the check. She was almost hysterical. He'd stolen the check from her and forged it.

I'm out $10,000. I was conned. I was a victim.

Or was I?

I could certainly consider myself a victim. But what does that do? A victim is angry. A victim is powerless. If I have no power, I can justify not taking any action. I can maintain my image of innocence regardless of the circumstances. I don't have to feel guilty for anything that happened to me. A victim does not produce anything of value.

If I decide to take responsibility for what happened, I'm accountable for my interpretations and my behavior. When I'm accountable, I'm oriented toward action and correction, rather than explanation and self-protection. When I take responsibility, I'm more interested in making something work than in making excuses for why something won't work.

Seen logically, and from a stance of responsibility, I deserved to lose that $10,000. I was greedy. I was careless. I never checked Michael's credentials or background. I gave him a check without demanding the completed paperwork first. When I got the check from someone I didn't know, I should have started inquiries.

Whether it's orange juice splattered all over the place or $10,000 winging off to Never-to-Be-Seen-Again Land, there are two ways of looking at any situation: You can be a victim or you can take responsibility. As a victim, you are powerless. When you take responsibility, you have power.

One of the keys to high achievement is choosing the perception that gives you power, the power to achieve.

For the loan reps at that San Diego mortgage company

there was plenty of "evidence" that they were too busy to prospect. That is the A side. How do they get to the B side? There were other loan reps at that company that were just as busy, had as many circumstances, priorities, interruptions, excuses, and stories, and still had the time to see 20 new contacts. The difference was in their point of view, the world they saw. Their paradigms were different.

What are paradigms? You might have already seen this, but let me borrow from an old example (Figure 8). With four straight lines, connect all nine dots.

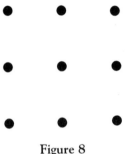

Figure 8

Figure 9 shows the solution. Most people try to solve this puzzle by keeping the four lines inside or on the unseen but *assumed* boundaries of the nine-dot square. The solution, however, lies *outside* the nine dots rather than inside.

A paradigm is an assumed method of doing things or of looking at things. It is "the way things are always done."

> **YOUR PERCEPTION MAY BE DIFFERENT**
> **FROM REALITY.**
> **THE TRUTH REALLY DOESN'T MATTER**

It is easy to get caught up in our circumstances and believe that our *perception* is reality. To our minds, truth does

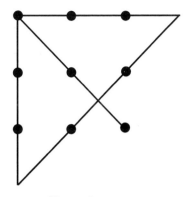

Figure 9

not count. What we *think* is true is what matters.

Our lenders had the time for prospecting, but because of human nature they did not see that time. We often do not see what is really there. Read this:

> You are quite literally unable to
> to perceive data right before your very eyes.

Read it again, pointing to every word. You'll notice the word *to* appears twice, one right after the other.

How could our loan reps have leveraged themselves to handle all of their priorities and still do what they said they would do? First, let's examine the second principle of human nature related to achievement.I call it "The Competition."

The Competition

Put a rat that hasn't been fed for three weeks in a box with two exits. One exit leads to a nice, comfortable pile of rags. The other exit leads to a mound of tasty food. Open the doors of both exits. The rat will rush to the food (Figure 10).

Now place a metal grid on the path to the food. Run a painful electrical current through the grid. Place the rat in

Rags   **Food**

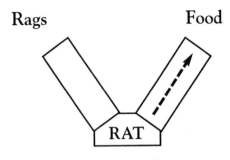

Figure 10

the box. He will rush toward the food, but when he hits the grid he'll turn right around and seek refuge in the rags (Figure 11).

Next, turn the electricity to the grid off, but leave the grid there. Now put the rat in the box again. He'll see the grid. He'll remember what happened the last time he stepped on it, and he'll go right for the rags. Hungry as he is, he won't even try to get to the food.

This is not just a conditioned reflex. This is an innate survival mechanism. In all organisms, including human beings, this survival mechanism instinctively recognizes the source of pain and—without any conscious thought at all—compels the organism to avoid that pain. Pain avoidance is an automatic response.

The rat avoids doing what he wants to do (eat) not be-

Rags   **Food**

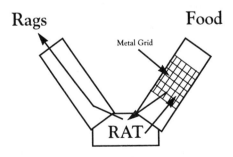

Figure 11

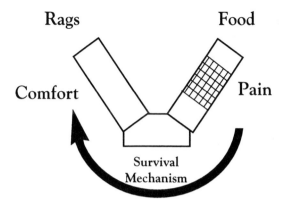

Figure 12

cause he is unable to do it but because of his perception that trying for that goal is painful. The rat is operating with a link that it has associated with that metal grid. It must avoid the possibility of pain that could kill it —not the *reality* of pain; the *possibility*.

Human beings have the same survival mechanism. If we do not do something we have committed to do, it's not because we're too busy, it's because the activity is somehow linked in our mind to pain.

THE SECOND LAW OF HUMAN NATURE:
We Avoid Pain and Seek Comfort

Where could prospecting be linked to pain for our loan reps? What bad thing could happen to them if they prospected? Consider this sign I saw in a real estate office one day: "Absolutely no loan agents in the office without a specific appointment. This means *you*." The pain the sales rep were avoiding was the pain of rejection—the word *no*. Our desire for approval is stronger than our desire for success and high achievement. The loan reps didn't *know* they would be rejected. They *thought* they might be rejected. And that was enough to prevent them from making their calls. Their natural survival mechanism did what it is supposed to do: It directed them from pain to comfort.

The Number One problem in commission sales is call reluctance. Here are some statistics:

> 80% of sales are made after the fifth "no."
> 48% of salespeople stop prospecting after the first "no."
> 20% continue until they get rejected a second time.
> 12% continue until they get a third "no," and then they stop.

80% of salespeople stop prospecting well short of the required number of "nos" for making a sale!

The Physiology of Rationalization

We don't always see all of reality, all of what is going on around us. This is another natural survival mechanism called *selective perception*. As with the survival mechanism of pain-avoidance, selective perception has its positive, life-saving side and its negative, achievement-killing side.

Some time ago, a rental house I own in Irvine, Calif., was vacant. I decided to install air conditioning and raise the rent before getting another tenant. Guess what I saw in the daily newspaper after making that decision. It seemed that suddenly, where I had never saw them before, there were ads for air conditioning on practically every page! What happened? Did the air-conditioning purveyors suddenly know I wanted air conditioning? Did the number of ads for air conditioning suddenly increase just when I made my decision? No. Before I wanted air conditioning, I ignored air-conditioning ads. Now that I was interested in it, I saw the ads. My selective perception had changed.

Another type of positive selective perception is in evidence when we fly a plane or drive a car. I remember my first flying lesson. The concept of steering a plane with my feet was foreign. I almost ran off the runway. The instructions from the tower came so fast and sounded so foreign, I couldn't make sense of them: "Cessna 634 November Foxtrot, you are cleared for an El Toro departure. Turn to 110 degrees immediately after takeoff, maintain VFR at or below 2,500 feet, contact 128.15 for radar advisories when cleared by tower to do so, squak 4560 and contact ground at 126.0." My flight instructor, however, repeated the instructions back to the tower with no problem. That was then. Today, because of familiarity, steering a plane with my feet is easy, and understanding tower instructions is second nature. I don't have to think about any of it. Selective perception lets me concentrate on the important things.

When I was a football coach at Cal State Fullerton, I bought a five-speed, stick-shift Honda Civic. I had never driven a car with a standard transmission before. Shifting the gears dominated my thinking at first. When I finally mastered the procedure, it became automatic. I didn't have to think, "Push in the clutch, put the gearshift *here*, let out the clutch . . . ." That was good because now I could pay attention to other things—such as the other cars on the road!

A recent experience of mine illustrates the negative side of selective perception. I was participating in a Total Quality Management training exercise that involved team-building using ropes. The exercise is a series of activities that involve risk: climbing, swinging, jumping from platforms onto trapezes, and other usually scary stuff.

My problem was that I had severely sprained my ankle three days before. The day after I sprained it, I had to fly to South Dakota for a speaking engagement, and I had to ask

for handicapped service—wheelchair and all—from the airline. I was on crutches and in excruciating pain during my
talk.

I went to the TQM training thinking there might be
something I could do even with my sprained ankle. I really
wanted to participate in these activities.

In the first exercise, the members of the group were
blindfolded and had to form a square with a rope. I wanted
to do that, but I wouldn't be able to stand for that long.

Next, the group was to navigate using blocks of wood of
various sizes across some cinder blocks. I couldn't do that. I
wouldn't be able to walk on those blocks of wood.

There was another activity involving walking on a wire
about three feet from the ground. Again, there was no way I
could do this, so I sat out.

Then it was time for lunch. *That* I could do!

After lunch came the high stuff: climbing trees, jumping.
I really wanted to do these exercises. I wanted to see
whether, even with my skydiving and flying experience, I
would have any fear; and if I did, whether I could conquer
it. But I just couldn't. My ankle was just too painful.

Now came an exercise where people went up a ladder,
then up a tree to a log, switched safety systems, walked on a
log 50 feet above the ground, climb over another wire and
make it to another platform. They were terrified!

My instructor asked if I wanted to try it. I started to say,
"No, thanks," but for some reason I said, "Yes."

What followed taught me a lesson. Not only was I able to
handle the weight on my foot, even though I favored one
side, I was able to do it faster than anyone else, with less effort, and with absolutely no fear at all. The lesson was this:
I had all the evidence that my sprained ankle would keep
me from participating that day, but the reality was the evidence was a lie. I *could* participate!

How does all of this apply to achievement in business?

For the loan reps, prospecting was linked to pain and they instinctively avoided it. This avoidance created a perceptual block: They did not see opportunities to prospect; they *rationalized* and and used selective perception to see only the reasons why they couldn't prospect.

Rationalization is a further defense mechanism of the brain and body.

To illustrate, ask yourself these questions:

1. Could you be more successful in your business, health and personal life than you are?
2. Do you know what you need to do to be more successful in those areas?
3. Are you doing everything you could be doing to be as successful as you could possibly be?

Even if you answered "yes" to all three questions, the chances are that you really don't believe it. Even if you don't believe it, however, you are not walking around feeling inadequate and depressed about your lack of performance compared to your capacity to perform. If you were, your self-image would be extremely low and your depression quite high.

Scientists have studied people who have stayed in depression for any prolonged period. They have found that the long-term depressed have a decreased white blood cell count. Here is where the defense mechanism of rationalization comes into play for most of us.

With a decreased white blood cell count, your immunity to disease is weakened. You will be more likely to fall ill and to stay ill. Illness is a threat to your survival. Your brain, which is created for survival, takes measures to prevent the depression that leads to the decreased white blood cell count that leads to illness. Your brain comes up with good reasons for your actions (or, more appropriately, your *lack of* action) so you will not feel depressed about it. That is rationalization. You have selective perception.

You don't see reality, you see only a portion of reality. You don't see opportunities to perform an uncomfortable activity; you see only reasons for not performing the activity.

> **RATIONALIZATION IS A
> JUSTIFICATION OF AVOIDANCE**

Why is it so difficult for millions of Americans to lose weight and keep it off? Is it because they don't know what to do or how to do it? No. The answer is simple: You diet and exercise. Then why is it so difficult? The reason is that the activities of dieting and exercising are linked to pain and deprivation. No matter how motivated a person may be, they will be compelled to avoid dieting and exercise because of that perception.

Let's look at this as it is related to a performance occupation such as sales (Figure 13). No matter what a person sells, these seven circles apply:

Figure 13

- To make money, you need to make sales.
- To make sales, you have to have a competitive product.
- To sell the product, you need to make presentations.
- To make presentations, you need to set appointments.
- To set appointments, you need to make calls.

• To make calls, you need to have an attitude that supports you in performing this sequence of activities.

Most people know what do do and how to do it. It is just a matter of getting themselves to take action that human nature is compelling them to avoid.

(In speaking of "attitude," I don't mean "positive mental attitude" [PMA]. PMA is a given among successful people; it is not what sets them apart. When I refer to attitude, I mean "point of view." When adversity strikes, I don't expect you to walk around saying, "Thank you for the adversity; every adversity leads to opportunity." I would expect you to handle the adversity, experience the emotions, then get back on track with productive activities.)

This all goes back to my first point: The way that you think effects your physiology and that determines what you will do. So if you want to increase your results in any area of your life, you need to take on perceptions that will give you the physiology that compels the action necessary to reach your desired outcome.

This is all about your point of view and having the flexibility to change your perception. The techniques I will share with you will enable you to do just that.

I need to ask for your help, as well: Be willing to let go of what is not working. Where in your life are you acting in a way that is not producing the results you really want? Where do you say and believe that you can't do something.

I am so glad I didn't listen to that inner voice that said, "I can't," at the TQM exercise, that inner voice I call The Alien.

If you saw the movie *Alien*, you'll recall the scene where the alien suddenly jumps up and grabs one of the crew members by the face and kills him. The "I can't" inner voice is like that alien. Put your hand firmly over your face. It's The Alien. It's got a grip on you that's hard to break, and it's trying to talk you out of performance.

When I said, "Yes," and got involved in the exercise, reached up and tore The Alien creature from my face and pushed it with all of its lying evidence away.

Stop doing what is not working. Stop listening to the lies of The Alien.

```
THE ALIEN IS A LIE!
```

Have you heard of how they catch monkeys in Africa? They put fruit in a vase and chain the vase to a fence. The monkey comes along, sees the fruit, and reaches in to get it. When he tries to get the fruit from the vase, the fist he makes by grasping it is too big to come back out. The monkey is now chained to the fence. Rather than letting go, the monkey keeps his grip on the fruit and is captured.

What Is High Achievement?

I am about to go against the grain of traditional American management philosophy and create a new paradigm of what it means to be a "high achiever." Let's start with the idea of commitment. Everyone falls somewhere from 0% to 100% on a continuum of commitment in the various areas of their lives (Figure 14)

In the years I have been doing training and research, I have found a profile shared by all low-commitment people. This profile fits both men and women. A low-commitment person is typically a second-income producer with a spouse who produces a large income. They are not concerned or driven by the dollar. They often have children in school who come home at 3 p.m., so they are not going to be out doing presentations or working after 3 p.m. They do not work evenings or weekends. If they accomplish anything,

100%

0

Figure 14

that's great. If not, they are just happy to have a place to go, something to do and people to talk with. Sound like anyone you know?

Contrast that person to the ultra-high-committed performer. This person is typically a single-income producer with high overhead. They have a mortgage on their home that needs to be paid even in a recession and even during the holidays (how rude!). This person has medical insurance payments, car insurance payments, children-in-college payments, expensive hobbies like flying and skydiving. They must make several thousand dollars each month just to break even. They will come in early, work late, work weekends. They will do whatever they can to be as successful as they can possibly be.

Now for the controversy. Most people would compare these two people and call the high-commitment person successful and a high achiever. But that is a myth left over from the 1980s. It fits the paradigm of evaluating by ranking and comparison.

EVALUATION BY RANKING
IS NOT RELEVANT

The late W. Edwards Deming, who was considered the guru of Japanese business, was quoted in a June 4, 1990, *Wall Street Journal* article:

> We are all born with intrinsic motivation, self esteem, dignity and an eagerness to learn. Our present system of management crushes that all out by replacing it with extrinsic motivation, by constantly judging people. We rank people with incentive pay, annual appraisals, production quotas. Judging people is not helpful. We can rank people according to height and of six people, one would one would be the tallest, one would be shortest. So what? You knew that before you started. That's the way business is run today. And it will get worse.

Deming is the creator of a concept called Total Quality Management (TQM), which was largely ignored until recently in this country. He went to Japan after the Second World War and taught this concept to the Japanese to help them in their rebuilding. In the United States, the philosophy has always been that making a profit is the only reason to be in business. Deming's philosophy is that you are in business , *first*, to provide jobs for people. The *second* reason to be in business is to stay in business. The *third* reason to be in business is to make a profit.

This is a dramatic paradigm shift. Does it work better than the old one? Look at the quality of what the Japanese are doing today and the direction they are headed.

Almost every corporation in the United States evaluates by ranking. I can go into any stockbroker's office and the branch manager can pull up on his computer today's production ranking of all of their sales reps. Real estate companies have national awards banquets where they honor their top producers. My question is, "Compared to what?"

It is not relevant to rank. Ranking does not tell you how effectively a person is operating. That low-commitment person doesn't want what the high-commitment person wants. They will not commit to do the same level of activity as the highly committed will.

But just because the high-commitment person does more than the low-commitment person doesn't mean that this person is more effective and producing higher quality. It just means that they are doing more than the other.

Using these ideas as a base, my definition of a high achiever is this:

> REGARDLESS OF YOUR LEVEL
> OF COMMITMENT, YOU ARE A HIGH
> ACHIEVER IF YOU DO WHAT YOU SAY
> YOU ARE GOING TO DO AND IF YOU
> ACHIEVE MAXIMUM RESULTS FROM
> YOUR EFFORTS

Using this definition, are low-commitment people high achievers? Yes. *If* they do what they say they are going to do and if they achieve maximum results from the effort.

The same applies to the highly committed. They are high achievers *only* if they do what they say they are going to do and achieve maximum return from their efforts. Forget evaluation by ranking and comparison. The *amount* of work is irrelevant.

This idea is totally foreign to most managers in this country. They often ask me how to handle a low-commitment person if you can't make comparisons. I tell them there are only two ways to handle the low-commitment person.

The first way is to call them into your office and say, "Good morning. You're fired." That's right. Don't get stressed over their low performance. If their performance doesn't meet your standards, get rid of them.

These managers will also ask how they can get the low-commitment person to become a high-commitment person. The answer is, "You can't." If you try to turn a low-commitment person into a high-commitment person, if you ask them to increase the amount of time they are willing to work, to increase the results of their work, you will only create a fear of change in their minds. They will resent it. Even if they are a high achiever by my definition, they will soon become a low achiever. And then you will have a good reason to fire them (which is probably what you wanted to do in the first place).

This brings us to the third major resistance that stands in the way of high achievement:

> **WE NATURALLY RESIST
> AND FEAR CHANGE**

Medical doctors call it *homeostasis*, from the Greek for "staying the same." It is the instinct to reject the foreign. A doctor transplants a new kidney into a patient. The patient's natural response is to reject this life-saving kidney because it is not the same as the body's other tissue. Psychologist call it *approach avoidance*: Start doing things that will lead to attaining a goal, get close, then "freak out" and sabotage yourself.

This creates a paradox. On the one hand, if you are over-weight and want to lose weight, you might be highly moti-vated. Losing weight is desirable and good. You go to semi-nars, you have great intentions, you have a great plan. On the other hand, losing weight will make you different from the way you are now. You will change. Your natural re-sponse is to avoid any activity that will threaten the status quo. You will fear and resist the change. You cannot reason with fear. Fear is not logical; it is emotional.

When it comes to business, making more money is desir-able. But this, too, is different—a change—so change-avoidance behavior comes into play.

Knowing this, what is the second way a manager can deal with a low-commitment person? Accept their level of com-mitment and coach them with this philosophy: "I accept your level of commitment. Now, how much more *effective* can you be within that level?" Focus on quality and effec-tiveness rather than on working harder. Ask the low-com-mitment person, "How much more in *results* can you get from the amount of time you are willing to put into your work?" This is a non-threatening approach that will not rouse his or her natural resistance to change.

The High Achiever's Point of View

Here is an alarming statistic. Only 2% of the population are high achievers. Most people who make a plan get side tracked by obstacles, circumstances, excuses, priorities, rea-sons, and stories, and get pulled away from the plan (Figure 15).

What is different about this 2%? Are they smarter? More motivated? More driven? Do they work harder? Is there something about them that others cannot hope to have? The answer is, "No!"

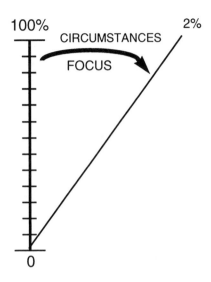

Figure 15

The difference is in their point of view. They have a point of view that compels them to action whereas most people have a point of view that compels them to avoidance and rationalizations.

Scientific research supports this claim. Whenever you measure any human variable—height and weight, dollars earned, I.Q., etc.—you will always find the results form a bell-shaped curve (Figure 16). I have rounded out and simplified the bell curve to illustrate my points.

First notice what I call the 2-7-2 rule. In any group of people, 2% will become the ultra-high achievers, 70% will be between +1 and -1 standard deviation from the average, and 2% will be the ultra-low achievers. The members of each of these groups are where they are on the curve because of their point of view.

The ultra-low achievers see how bad things are. Taking the situation in California at the time this is written, they see IBM laying off 25,000 employees across the nation. They see one company moving to Arizona, which puts

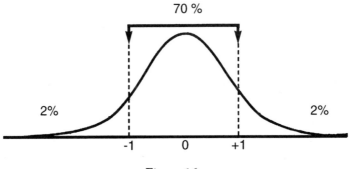

Figure 16

2,000 Californians out of work. Another company moves to Nevada, affecting 1,000 employees. Military bases at Long Beach, El Toro, and San Diego are closing down, which affects the economy. Interest rates are at a 27-year low, but these people notice only that the housing market is still in a slump. They see doom and gloom everywhere. Dr. Kevorkian the "Suicide Doctor" is the most sought after speaker in California!

Real estate agents in this 2% are not likely to go to their offices in the evening with a cross-reference index and make CMA calls to set listing appointments. Why should they? After all, if they get a listing, it's only going to be overpriced and won't sell. It will cost them over $500 to market and advertise the listing. They will lose money. What's the use? Do you think they will send a mail-out in their territory? Again, why even try? What's the use.

This example is drawn from true life. While doing a needs assessment for a commercial real estate group in San Diego preparatory to my giving a full-day training session, I was told that in 1992 there were 900 brokers in the area. When I did the assessment, there were only 400. This company's agents saw the overbuilding in the area and saw the Resolution Trust Corporation dumping undervalued properties on the market. They gave up and just stopped working.

There was business out there, but it required focused and concentrated effort.

Will the techniques in this book help this group. Absolutely. Will they seek the help? Absolutely not. In their minds, there is nothing they can do. The entire situation is caused by Congress or by the White House or by the capital gains tax or by . . . .

**THE POINT OF VIEW SHARED BY
LOW ACHIEVERS IS:
IT'S NO USE—I MIGHT AS WELL GIVE UP**

How about the 70% in the middle? Their shared viewpoint is shown by Figure 17.

What is the real problem here? Hint: The real problem is not what is obvious. True, they have the tools (round wheels) to be more successful at their task and they are not using them, but that is not the real problem. The real problem is that *they are successfully moving the cart the way it is!* They are following the old paradigm and adage: If it isn't broken, don't fix it.

It seems absurd to operate so ineffectively when the tools for dramatic improvement are so readily available. Well, welcome to the real world. These people do not realize there is anything wrong. They are successful. If you told them they could be more successful, they would deny it. And that's the word I use to describe this group: Denial.

I don't use "denial" in a negative way. I simply mean they are not aware that there is anything wrong or that they could be doing better than they are. They are locked into their comfort zones and justify their successes and failures. This situation reminds me of Alcoholics Anonymous. A person at an AA meeting introduces himself with "Hello.

Figure 17

My name is So-and-So and I am an alcoholic." By doing so, they acknowledge—they do not deny—they have a problem with alcohol. For the average achievers, just as for alcoholics, denial and rationalization are the biggest competitors against achievement.

Can I help this group? Of course, but they must be ready to position themselves for the next level in their lives. They must stop denying that they can do better.

**THE POINT OF VIEW SHARED
BY AVERAGE ACHIEVERS IS:
DENIAL**

What about the high achievers? There is only one thing that separates them from the rest. It's not talent or ability or drive. It *is* viewpoint, but a very special one.

Have you ever been around someone who is the best at what they do? When I was in graduate school I was a graduate-assistant coach in both football and wrestling. I had the opportunity to coach Jeff Blatnick, who overcame Hodgkin's disease to win a Gold Medal at the 1984 Olympics. (He also carried the flag for the United States at the closing ceremonies, an honor voted on by the athletes themselves.)

I worked with Jeff almost every day for two years. He wasn't the biggest athlete. In fact, he was usually smaller than his opponent, and he was usually not as strong. Yet, Jeff was unbeatable. Not that I was responsible for that. Jeff was *my* teacher about high achievement. Working with him for as long as I did helped me to understand the mind of someone who is the best in the world at what they do.

What was Jeff's attitude? Did he ever think, "Who is this guy Bob Davies, who only wrestled for one year at Rutgers University. What makes him think he can be of help to me? I'm already the best in the world."? No; that is not how Jeff thought. Did he ever think, "Why do I have to do this basic drill? I am so much better than the rest of the team."? Again, the answer is no.

He did everything we asked everyone else to do. Then, what were Jeff's thoughts? Jeff's point of view was that he knew that he was good, but he also knew he had limitations and needed all the coaching he could get. He recognized the value and need for coaching. He knew he could not do it alone and that he had limitations that he needed to overcome. Jeff knew that to reach his goals he needed to compensate for his limitations. That is the point of view shared by high achievers.

**THE POINT OF VIEW SHARED BY HIGH ACHIEVERS IS:
I HAVE LIMITATIONS
AND I MUST COMPENSATE FOR THOSE LIMITATIONS**

High achievers are not in denial. They don't think they have it made. They don't view themselves as having arrived. They acknowledge their successes and are driven to a higher level of performance. Self-actualization drives them. Reaching their potential drives them. The idea of learning more, of being coached to a higher level, drives them.

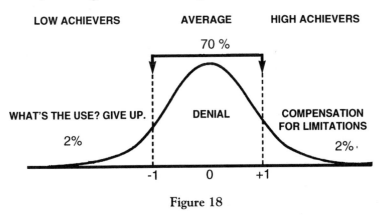

Figure 18

What is compensation? I most often fly a Cessna 172. This is a single-engine aircraft, and as the propeller spins clockwise, Newton's Third Law of Motion ("For every action there is an equal and opposite reaction") goes into effect. The spin of the propeller makes the aircraft constantly want to turn left.

I have to compensate for this left-turning tendency. If, for example, I take off from John Wayne Airport in Orange County with the intention of landing at Lindbergh Field in San Diego and I don't compensate for this left-turning tendency, I'll get to what I think is my destination, land, and see a sign reading "Welcome to Montgomery Field" (another airport 10 miles east of Lindbergh).

The plane does what its design demands: It naturally drifts to the left. And that is what all organisms—including human beings—and machines will do—what they are designed to do.

For me to get this plane to do what I want it to do, I need to compensate for its natural design. I compensate by stepping on the right rudder pedal. This turns the tail fin (rudder) to the right, compensating for the air flow and torque, keeping the aircraft in straight and level flight. I can get the aircraft to do what I want it to do rather than what it is designed to do, but only if I compensate for it's natural design.

The same thing is true for human beings. As we've discovered so far in this book, we are designed to avoid doing things that we don't feel comfortable doing. We are designed to avoid activities that we have linked to being uncomfortable, and then to rationalize. We are designed to resist, to fear, and to avoid change.

If left alone, we will do all of that. Our achievements will be the best we can do, given our rationalizations and avoidances. If we work hard, this will usually put us right in the middle of the bell curve. For us to be high achievers, regardless of our level of commitment, we must compensate for our limitations.

> **IF LEFT ALONE, ALL ORGANISMS
> AND MACHINES
> WILL DO EXACTLY WHAT
> THEY ARE DESIGNED TO DO**

The Actions of High Achievers

How do the high achievers compensate for their limitations?. They use a strategy that is at the core of the system that will be explained in the rest of this book:

> **THE COMMON DENOMINATOR OF HIGH
> ACHIEVERS:
> THEY SET GOALS
> AND HAVE A METHOD OF
> REINFORCEMENT AND SUPPORT
> TO HELP REACH THOSE GOALS**

Simple, isn't it? This is the common thread that puts the elite where they are. Of course, they need talent and ability. Of course, they need to work, but there are people all over the bell curve who work harder than they do and and are more talented but not as successful. This operating principle separates the elite from the rest.

You might think that by including goals in the formula for high achievement that I've contradicted my earlier assertion that goal setting does not work, that it is an incomplete process. Goal setting *by itself* does not work. What does work is a complete strategy that adds reinforcement and support to goal setting. Reinforcement and support are major factors in this system. This strategy will produce immediate results in all areas of your life.

Human nature and The Alien will compete with you and try every illusion possible to trick you into not using the strategy that follows because this system is in direct conflict with human nature. It will be easier to sit back, keep things the way they are, and not change. But if you accept the challenge to excel, then let this exciting lifetime competition with yourself begin.

Chapter 3
The Solution

We have found that human nature stands in the way of high achievement because of three natural resistances:

1. You will resist doing what you do not feel like doing.
2. We avoid pain and seek comfort.
3. We naturally resist and fear change.

The system I have developed actually *uses and redirects* these survival mechanisms to create thoughts, feelings, and actions that lead to high achievement. It is done in four phases, or steps:

Phase I GOALS AND ACTIVITIES	**Phase II** IDENTIFY CIRCUMSTANCES. WHAT WOULD STOP ME?
Phase III CHANGE MY PLAN OR CHANGE MY THINKING AND NEGOTIATE	**Phase IV** CREATE INTERNAL AND EXTERNAL SUPPORT

1. Setting goals and identifying activities.

2. Identifying the circumstances that would stand in your way.

3. Changing your plan or changing your thinking (negotiating).

4. Creating internal and external support.

You've heard it all before: You cannot hit a target you cannot see or don't have; you can't build a house without a blueprint. So I'm not going to go into goal-setting theory or philosophy. I'm going to go directly to Phase I, "Goals and Activities."

If someone were to put a whole, roasted elephant on the table and tell you your job was to eat it, you'd probably be overwhelmed by the size of the job. An elephant is huge! How would you go about doing it? There's only one way: Take one bite at a time.

The same is true of goals, goal setting, and goal achievement. You achieve your goals one bite at a time. If you set a huge goal for yourself and try to get it all in one bite, you're going to choke on it. You won't achieve your goal, and you'll start making up all sorts of excuses for not achieving it.

That's why, with this system, we set monthly goals. Then we determine what activities must be done each *week* to reach those goals. Then we break the weekly activities into daily activities—chewable bites.

Let's use just one example. Suppose your monthly goal is to phone 500 prospects this month. Breaking that goal into four weeks gives you 125 calls to make each week. If your work week is five days, you will have to make 25 calls a day. The idea of 25 calls is a lot easier to handle than 500, isn't it?

One bite at a time.

Another reason for breaking our goal into weekly bites is

that we are going to formulate a weekly reinforcement technique. This is because research has shown that human beings must have frequent reinforcement, and a month between reinforcement events is too much time. This reinforcement is very important for achieving specific results.

So the first thing to do is make a copy of the weekly time calendar in Appendix C. If you don't have access to a copying machine right now, draw a copy on a piece of paper (make a year's worth of photocopies later).

You have to have a clear and visual awareness of your available time and time commitments for the next week. Begin by blocking out the appointments and any commitments that you already know you have for the next seven days.

(There is something magical about the number seven. There are seven digits in a phone number, seven is the lucky number in Vegas. There are seven days in a week and that is our focus. I encourage you to have five-year plans, yearly goals, and quarterly goals. Just as in eating the elephant, however, these must be broken down into more workable monthly and weekly commitments. *A seven-day plan produces great power.*)

Breaking the seven-day plan into even more manageable periods of time—ranging from five minutes to an hour—creates even more power because you know what you are going to do. You will not be drifting at sea, wondering what comes next.

TIME AWARENESS IS POWER

This method of blocking out time was used when I was a football coach at Cal State Fullerton. We left nothing to chance. Each two-and-one-half-hour practice session was broken down into five-minute increments. Here is an example of how my practice card might have looked for one of those sessions:

2:00-2:10	Team stretching
2:10-2:15	Individual unit agility drills
2:15-2:20	Unit tackling drills
2:20-2:30	Unit-OLB vs San Jose State corner blocking schemes
2:30-2:40	OLB vs tight end man-to-man coverage
2:40-2:55	Man-to-man coverage vs offense TE and X for Cover 3 double coverage
2:55-3:15	With inside LB vs scout team San Jose State inside blocking schemes
3:15-3:20	Break
3:20-3:45	7-on-7 skeleton pass coverage vs offense (scripted- 20 plays)
3:45-4:10	Defensive game plan vs San Jose State scout team offense (scripted)
4:10-4:25	Special teams, kick-off, kick-off return, hands team
4:25-4:35	Conditioning-overview, Titan huddle

You'll notice we didn't decide what we were going to do as we went along. We created a model of the way we wanted practice to go and then just followed our model. Our manager would blow a horn at five-minute intervals. I looked at my practice card and knew where I needed to be and what I had planned to do for that block of time.

Being aware of time gives you the illusion of slowing time down. If you ever get into a performance rut, make yourself script your day in five- to 15-minute intervals. Be accountable to your time. You should be able to account for every minute for an entire day.

Once you block out your time commitments for the next seven days, you have a visual representation of how much time you have available. Now you can start to make decisions on what activities you want to commit to and when. First, let's take a look at a method we're going to use to help you plan your goals and activities. It's called "Mind Mapping" because it helps you visualize and make associations in the same way your brain does.

Phase I: Setting Goals and Activities

In setting goals and the activities necessary to meet those goals, we are going to use a method called *mind mapping* (also known as *neural mapping*) because it increases your creativity and helps you use more of your brain's power and potential in planning. It taps into the creative right side of your brain. We will discuss the two sides of the brain further when we discuss the conscious and subconscious minds later, but, for now, suffice it to say that we live in a linear, left-brain society. Lists are a left-brain method. Through the use of a mind map, which is more of a picture than a list, you will stimulate the right side of your brain, which would otherwise be dormant during planning. By writing on the mind map, you will stimulate the left brain. The advantage is an increase in creativity and access to more information for planning—*whole-brain* planning.

The reason is that, although we're taught to take notes in a linear (left-brain) way, the brain actually works in a three-dimensional way. It puts bits of information in different parts of itself. It makes associations between and among these bits of information.

Recent research in the way people recognize objects they see supports this contention. For example, if you look at an apple on a picnic table 10 feet away, the image is transmitted along your optic nerve to a spot in your cortex where it is literally mapped onto the surface of your brain tissue just as it appears.

Now your brain examines the various attributes of that image: edges, contours, color, and so on. This information is sent to the temporal lobe of the brain, where different cells make different comparisons and associations. The apple is red and round, so cells programmed with red, round associations are stimulated. The information is also sent to another part of the brain that decides how far the apple is from you (this is the area of the brain that says, "Duck!" if the apple were to be thrown at you).

When these cells have done their work, they send information to yet another area of the brain where associative memories are stored. If the information finds a "match" in the associative memory area (Aha! It's an apple!), your brain tells you, "It's an apple. It tastes like this, it smells like this, it has seeds" and so on.

Here's an interesting result of that research that is most important for our purposes: Images formed in the brain follow the exact same paths, but in reverse! As reported in one article about this research, "Information flows richly in both directions at all times."

This supports the idea that I have emphasized before: The subconscious accepts as being true that which is vividly imagined. The subconscious mind cannot tell the truth from a lie. It cannot tell the difference between what is real and what we think is real.

You don't have to fully understand mind mapping to be able to use and and reap its benefits. Simply by making notes in the mind-map format you will stimulate both sides of your brain. Use it now. Figure 19 is a mind map that shows you how.

As an example, I've created a quick mind map of my life, which is shown as Figure 20. You can see that I start with the major themes of my life: birth, early schooling, high school, college, first job, graduate school, second job, third

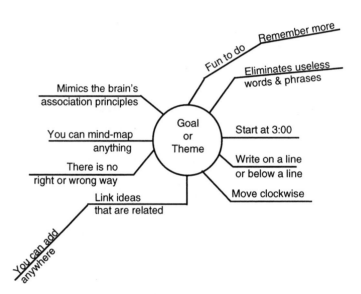

Figure 19

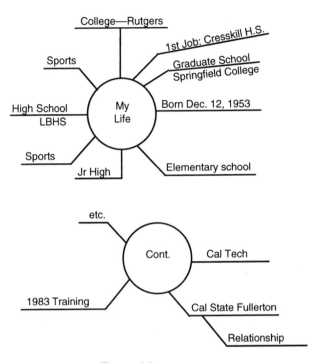

Figure 20

job, career change, etc. As offshoots, I would add sports, friends, relationships, and the like. Once I fill in the major themes I come back and am more specific.

For practice, you might like to do the same thing. Figure 21 gives you a start.

The next step is obvious: Sit down in a quiet area and allow yourself some undisturbed time. You must answer this very important question:

What Do I Want?

In the center of a blank sheet of paper, draw a circle about the size of a quarter. In the center of the circle, write "What do I Want?" Now, at 3 o'clock on the circle, draw a line about an inch long and write on that line the first

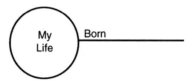

Figure 21

thing that comes to your mind when you ask yourself, "What do I want?"

Think in terms of the categories shown in the diagram and list on the next page.

Don't make any judgments. Freely brainstorm and put down any idea, however foolish or unrealistic it might seem.

Now answer a second very important question:

What Do I Need to Do to Get What I Want?

For example, if you want to lose 50 pounds, you will need to exercise and diet. You will need to change some habits and attitudes. If you are in a relationship that you want to improve, you will have to spend more time together, go to dinner, visit with friends, and so on.

Once you have asked yourself those two questions (What do I want? and What do I have to do to get what I want?) you are almost ready to begin the journey to what I call a behavioral contract. First, however, you must go from the vague to the very specific.

I am now going to show you how to have precise communication with yourself. You have to have specific and measurable actions to which you can be held accountable. It is not good enough to say, "I am going to prospect," or "I am going to diet," or "I am going to be more patient." You have to establish what will be the evidence of those vague goals. The way to do this is by using a *precision probing model*. It is illustrated as the outline of a hand and fingers in Figure 22.

The precision probing model is adapted from Neuro-Linguistic Programming (NLP). The founders of this therapy, Bandler and Grinder, studied therapists such as Fritz Pearls, Virginia Satir, and Milton Erickson, who achieved dramatic and quick results with their clients. They found that we human beings do three things with our daily communication

GOAL CATEGORIES

Physical ....Develop and maintain a high level of energy. Consistent physical exercise. Six to seven hours of sleep per night.

Stress control ....Ability to resist illness and disease. Fear and anxiety causes muscles to contract and blood vessels to constrict. Illness sets in when blood cannot be delivered freely to the body's tissues, providing oxygen, nutrients, and antibodies.

Nutritional ....Habit of eating nutritious foods. Observation of calories, low fat, low sodium, low refined flour and sugar diet.

Mental ....Vivid imagination of goals. Positive attitude and setting of conditions. Effective use of the limiting conscious mind. Do it now!

Emotional ....Confronting and conquering fear. Change adversity to opportunity. Ability to perceive constructive feedback as positive to change. Ability to turn rejection into enthusiasm.

Financial ....Money flows. Dollar sense.

Educational ....Constantly seeking opportunities to have the academic competitive edge. Reading, tapes, etc.

Family....................An appreciation of those you love.

Social ....Build warm and lasting relationships.

Spiritual.................Direction of purpose plus energy to fulfill purpose. Sense of Higher Self.

with ourselves and with others:

1. We delete;
2. We distort; and
3. We generalize.

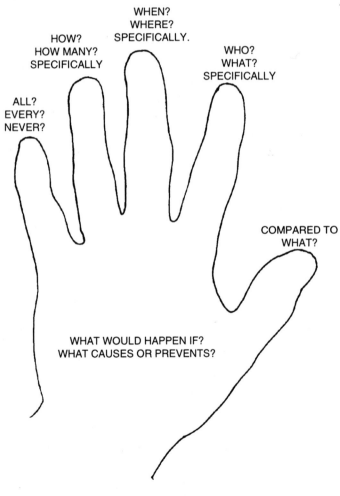

Figure 22

Consider this example: Mary is recently divorced. She is in great pain. Nothing seems to be going right in her life. She has even thought about suicide. Mary goes to a therapist, who is schooled in the use of the precision probing model.

Mary begins by saying, "I'm just so depressed".

The therapist responds with, "*What or who specifically* is depressing you?"

Mary says,"No one will ever love me like my ex-husband John did."

The therapist asks, "*Nobody?*"

Mary says, "Well, people just don't respect me like they used to."

The therapist asks, "*Who specifically* is not respecting you?"

Mary answers, " Well, John in my office has been treating me rudely."

The therapist asks, "*When specifically* has John treated you rudely?"

Mary says, "The other day at lunch John made a remark about . . . ."

You can see that the therapist has guided Mary from the general "No one will ever love me like my ex-husband did," to identifying *specific* problems with a *specific* person. This forces Mary to make a psychological shift and identify what is really bothering her so she can confront it and make a decision about it.

Refer to Figure 23. Every time the therapist challenges a generalization, which is a violation of the precision model, the client is forced to go into a deeper awareness of the whole situation. The deeper the awareness, the lower the pain.

The precision probing model can be used as a great sales tool. Have you ever had a client give you an objection that

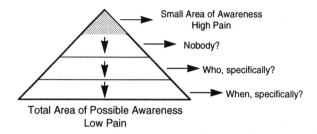

Figure 23

made you feel like killing the client. (Don't do that, it just destroys rapport if you murder your client).

Let's use the model for this objection in a real estate sales situation: "I have to talk to some other people before I can make a decision." The wrong response would be to angrily respond, "What's wrong with you? Can't you make up your own mind?. Who is going to live in the house, you or other people? Are you a wimp? Are you going to buy or not? Why live?!"

It has been scientifically proven that this kind of a response does not lead to referrals. Why not use the precision model?

"*Who, specifically,* do you need to talk to?"
"*How many* people, *specifically*, do you need to talk to?
"*When, specifically*, will you talk to these people?"
"If you didn't need to talk to other people, would this be the right house for you?"
And so on.

What a difference! You now become a great therapist. Every time you use this you create psychological shifts in your clients. Every time? That's right! Make it second nature to challenge any violations of the precision model (*every time* is a form of *always*).

As an example of how to use this precision probing model in setting your goals and activities, look at Figure 24, a mind map for losing weight.

It is not enough to say, "I will exercise." Using the precision probing model, you ask yourself, "When will I exercise?" You might not know exactly when, but you can commit to three times this week. "Where will I exercise?" At the gym I belong to. "What type of exercise?" Weight training and running. "For how long will I run?" Four to five miles.

It is not good enough to say "I am going to diet." What does it mean to diet? For example, in the part of the mind map where I've written "Eat fruits and veggies," you would use the precision probing model to pin that activity down in terms of how much and when. When you use the precision probing model, you go from the vague to the specific. You can measure four servings of fruit five days this week. Where it says I eat too much, it is not acceptable to commit to eating less. I need to take that desire and put it into an

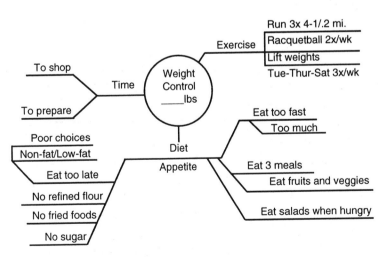

Figure 24

observable and measurable activity for the next seven days. Perhaps I then commit to eating only one portion of a particular size four times this week at dinner. At the end of the week I can be held accountable by my partner, who would ask me if I went three evenings without having seconds at dinner ("partnering," which is an integral part of this system, will be explained in great detail later).

Now I create another mind map based on my answers to the precision probing model (Figure 25).

Notice how, although I'm specific about what I'm going to do and how much I'm going to do it, I've also built in some flexibility. We all know that if you set a rigid schedule for yourself, real life will sooner or later make sure it's disrupted. That's one of the problems with traditional goal setting: You are told to make schedules and stick to them. When you can't stick to the schedule, you give up.

For example, what if you were to commit to making cold calls on the phone on Friday from 6 p.m. to 9 p.m. and an out-of-town buyer unexpectedly shows up on Friday at 6 p.m. Are you going to say, "Sorry, I can't work with you today. I promised to make cold calls at this time."? Of course not!

To build flexibility, you would commit to making a total of three hours of cold calls that week, rather than at a specific time (unless you *must* do it at a specific time). You can plan to do it on Friday, but if you can't, you can still make the calls on Saturday and fulfill your commitment.

On my weight-loss mind map I've allowed myself the same type of flexibility. I promise to go to the gym every day, but I give myself the options of either 5:30 a.m. or 6 p.m. I promise to cut back on diet drinks by limiting myself to having them only two times a week. I don't promise to have them only on Tuesday and Thursday. I have to allow for my being human. If I absolutely crave a diet drink on Monday, I'm going to have it, knowing I can have only one

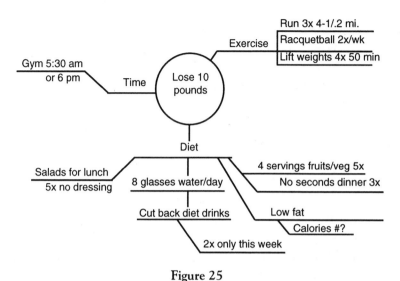

Run 3x 4-1/.2 mi.
Racquetball 2x/wk
Lift weights 4x 50 min
Exercise
Gym 5:30 am
or 6 pm
Time
Lose 10
pounds
Diet
Salads for lunch
5x no dressing
8 glasses water/day
4 servings fruits/veg 5x
No seconds dinner 3x
Cut back diet drinks
Low fat
Calories #?
2x only this week

Figure 25

more sometime this week.

From the entries on my weight-loss mind map, I now create statements about them, as follows. These are the statements I will record on a special audiotape, which I will explain about in detail later.

> I am loved, safe, secure, sexy and aroused as I weigh _____ pounds or less in _____.
> My stomach is hard and my sides are slim and trim. I am in great shape as I weigh _____ pounds or less.

> I thrive on exercise. Exercise makes me successful in all aspects of my life. As I love all people I do exercise.

> I run at least _____ times per week for at least _____ miles per run. I love to run and I do. I love the feeling in my legs as I effortlessly run. It is beautiful and relaxing as I do run.

I play racquetball at least _____ times per week. Racquetball releases chemicals in my body that keep me healthy and energetic. I am addicted to racquetball.

I lift weights every _____, _____ and _____ of every week forever. I love the feeling of being slim and trim and in great shape. I hear the compliments that people give me because I am slim, trim, and in great shape.

Hunger is my friend. When I feel hungry I recognize that this is my body's way of thanking me for keeping us healthy. I eat only when I am hungry and only the amounts that I need to stay completely healthy. I am completely healthy.

I eat only foods that are good for me. My subconscious mind uses only the amounts of calories that I need to maintain perfect health and I am in perfect health.

When I am hungry, I eat all of the fruits and vegetables that I want. Fruits and vegetables satisfy my hunger and taste great. I feel full when I eat fruits and vegetables.

I am always on a diet. I take great pride as I have great control of my eating habits because I desire the feeling of being slim, trim, and in great shape. I hear the compliments that people give me because I am slim, trim, and in great shape.

I chew my food slowly, enjoying it thoroughly. I chew my food slowly, less food tastes great. I am an efficient eating machine. I am a lean, effective, healthy person.

I eat non-fat foods at all times. I eat only foods that are good for my body.

I eat only up until 10 p.m. I take great pride in going to bed hungry. As I hug _____ I love to go to bed hungry. As I make money and have a successful career, I love to go to bed hungry.

I take time to shop and prepare foods for myself. When I eat out, I eat salads and other low-fat and well-prepared foods.

Having created these statements, I ask myself whether I would be likely to reach my goal of losing x pounds if I did everything I'm committing myself to. If the answer is "no," then what else do I need to do? Suppose the answer is "yes." The next step is Phase II, "Identify Circumstances: What Would Stop Me?"

Phase II: What Would Stop Me?
The next step is to look at what you have chosen as goal-achieving activities and about each of them ask yourself, "What would stop me from doing this?" Make a mind map of your answers, as I have in Figure 26 about my weight-loss activities.

Let's look at one example of what would stop me from dieting: "I *like* the taste of food". It would be absurd for me to commit to dieting without realizing this attitude on my part and doing something to alter it. If I don't do something about my feeling toward food, my diet won't last. The instinct of avoiding pain (eating less) and seeking comfort (eating as I have been doing) is far more powerful than my desire to lose weight.

**THE INSTINCT TO AVOID IS
MORE POWERFUL
THAN THE DESIRE TO ACHIEVE**

To combat the things that would stop you from performing your goal-achieving activities, you start by making statements that are their opposites, as in the following list based on my "what would stop me" mind map:

1. I love to run and I do. Running is healthy for me. Running helps me to make a lot of money and I do run and make money. Running helps me to reach my goals and to love other people and I do run and reach my goals and love other people.

2. I love to get up early and I do. I take pride that I am doing something that most people won't do. I love the darkness as I run. I love the chill in the air.

3. My knees feel great all the time. I have a healthy blood flow in them and they work great. My entire body is healthy.

4. I exercise for life. I exercise for the rest of my life. I think only of today's workout. Here and now!

5. When I eat foods that have a taste I love, I find that I get filled up very quickly. I crave salads. I crave salads. I crave salads.

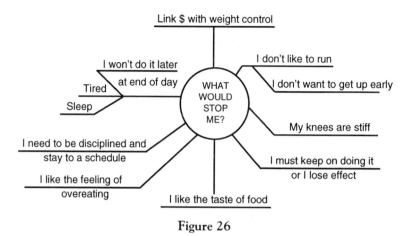

Figure 26

6. I am disciplined. I stay on my exercise and diet schedule.

7. Whenever I have a thought that does not support my workout and diet, I immediately destroy that thought. I have only positive thoughts that forward the action. If my thoughts don't help me, I stop thinking and just do.

8. I always have energy. I always have great workouts.

9. I sleep soundly all the time. I sleep soundly all the time. My body needs only _____ hours of sleep.

10. As I make money and reach my goals, I stay on my program.

Look at statement No. 5. This statement creates a relationship between eating and quickly feeling full. I am also programming in the command that I love salads and that I crave them.

When you create the statements that will combat the things that would get in the way of performing the goal-achieving activities, don't worry about whether they are true. What you believe is true does not matter. Your subconscious mind accepts as being true whatever is vividly imagined or suggested. You will respond regardless of "reality."

Once you have determined what you think you are willing to commit to for the next seven days, you are ready to write your *behavioral contract*, a copy of which you will give or send to your partner, or the contents of which you can convey over the phone. Use the form on the next page for this.

Phase III: Change Your Plan or Change Your Thinking

When you have identified what could prevent you from carrying through with your activities, ask yourself,"Are these reasons for not doing something valid? Given these reasons, do I still want *x*?"

If the reasons are valid, you will have to change your plan. If the reasons are not valid, you will have to change your thinking if you expect to achieve the goal.

This is a realistic approach. If the resistance is real and valid, change your plan. If you still want to achieve your goal, find another route. If you find you really don't want to attain a particular goal, forget it. Striving for something you really don't want will only waste your physical and psychic energy. You won't get it (your mind will put up resistance against having it), you will feel guilty about not getting it, and you will fall into that old familiar routine of rationalization.

For example, when my seminar business grew to the point where I would have to travel, I had to negotiate with myself so I would not resist being on the road. The reason was that I wanted to be with my daughter Danielle as much as possible. So when I had the opportunity to give a seminar in either Hawaii or San Francisco, I chose San Francis-

NAME

GOALS AND ACTIVITIES FOR WEEK OF _____TO _____

Partners and Contact Numbers

_____

_____

_____

_____

_____

MY VISIONS ARE	
Family	_____
Spiritual	_____
Physical	_____
Business/Financial	_____
Educational	_____
Recreational	

My Number One Priority Accomplishment This Month Is:	My Key Goal for This Month:

My Promises/Goals for the Week Are:

1	
2	
3	
4	
5	
6	
7	
8	
9	
10	
11	
12	
13	
14	
15	
16	
17	
18	

co. I would have enjoyed Hawaii, but it's a five-hour trip, and that would separate me from Danielle for too long. San Francisco was only an hour's flight, so I could be home on the weekend to be with Danielle. If I had chosen Hawaii, my mind would have set up resistance. Instead, I changed my plan (instead of changing my thinking). By negotiating with myself, I came up with a plan that lets me accept being on the road.

Phase Four: Creating Leverage with External and Internal Support

We have already taken the idea of goal setting much farther than most people do. We have made goals and goal-achieving activities truly realistic by examining them, by determining what might stop you from accomplishing them, and by asking whether you *really* want what you said you wanted.

Once all that is done, you can proceed to the most powerful part of this entire system: support (both internal and external) and accountability.

This part of the system is what makes the difference between mere intentions and performance. I might *say* I am going to eat salads, and I might *commit* to eating five salads this week, but without a method of internal support (changing my belief about being hungry all the time and not liking salads) and accountability to someone else (a "partner"), the likelihood of my doing what I say I'm going to do is slim.

External Support

Your external support is a partner (or partners) who will hold you accountable for what you say you are going to do. This "partnering" is based on the "master mind" principle: two or more people who voluntarily come together and creatively put their combined energy behind a major purpose.

Practice has shown that a master-mind group will accomplish much more than any one of them could do individually.

Partnering uses blended mind power in action to obtain unlimited results. None of us can be totally successful alone. We need other people to energize our outlook and find the best that is in us.

Greatness is dependent on two or more people working together. You can more easily create positive results in your life when you are open to looking at yourself , your problems and your opportunities from another's point of view.

Another way of saying this is to have coaching in your life. Great athletes all have coaches. They know that it takes another individual to stretch them beyond their self-perceived boundaries. When someone else holds you to as high or higher an expectation than you hold yourself, breakthroughs occur.

**UNITED WE STAND
DIVIDED WE FALL**

Who should you pick for a support partner? Find the toughest, no-nonsense, lowest-empathy person you know; someone who will stand strong for you and hold you accountable for what you say you will do; someone who will not let you escape with petty excuses, reasons, stories, circumstances, and rationalizations. Remember: There are no excuses, there are only results. The most important aspect of strategic planning and accountability through partnering is the accountability that comes from knowing that someone is going to check up on you and will expect you to do what you said you would do over the next seven days. Do you have someone in mind? Give them a copy of this book so they can share the same enthusiasm as you do.

People will often want to choose their spouse as a partner. Although many professional coaches hold the opinion that spouses are not the best choice, and my experience has shown that they are often correct, I suggest you try your spouse as a partner if you want to. If it is producing results, continue. You be the judge. (By the way, if you find that you are not successful with finding a support partner and want to be in my paid professional coaching program, call 714-854-1426 for details.)

Partnering Ground Rules

(For the purpose of this example, the seven-day period will be Monday through Sunday evening.)

1. Telephone call to partner every seventh day or evening. The objective of the call is to evaluate the accuracy of performance versus intended performance, pay fines and to recommit for the next seven days.

2. You have until two days from the time of the expected call to get your goals into your partner. If, in this example, your goals are not communicated to your partner by Tuesday, it is an automatic fine of $20.

3. Be ready for your Sunday night, 9 p.m. call. Have your goals for the next seven days ready and be clear about what happened and why you fell short of your expectations if you did from last week.

4. Make sure that your commitments for the next seven days include the paying of your fines.

5. Fines for not doing what you said you would do are $5. No bartering, trading or excusing. It is not okay not to ac-

cept the payment of fines. It is an important part of the program. You are not being a nice guy when you forgive the fine, you are being selfish.

6. Be support for each other to stretch yourselves beyond what you think your comfort zone level is. Be reasonable, but also be challenging. Limited risk equals limited gain.

7. Decide what to do with your fine money. You could send it to each other and simply keep it. You might opt to pool the fine money and give it to a charity, or donate to some non-reward cause. A non-reward cause might be a competitor who you don't want to help. The only way to avoid this aversion is to do what you said you would do and therefore have no fines.

When you present your list of commitments for the week, your partner should use the precision probing model if your activities are too vague (and you should do the same for your partner's list of commitments).

For example, if I were to have a goal of improving my relationship with someone who we'll call Gail for the purpose of this illustration, the conversation might go like this:

Mike: "What do you mean, specifically, when you say you want to improve the relationship? Compared to what? How would you measure an improved relationship? How can I hold you accountable to this? How would you know at the end of the week if you improved your relationship?"

Me: "Well, I would know by the way I would feel and how we relate to each other".

Mike: What specific activities are you going to commit to that would improve your relationship?

Me: I've already thought about that. Here is what I commit to over the next seven days (Figure 27).

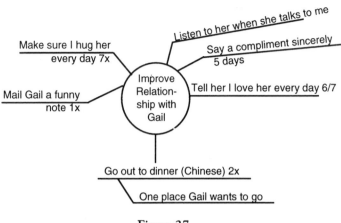

Figure 27

Mike: How would you measure listening to Gail when she talks to you?

Me: I will make a conscious note of where my mind is. I know that this is somewhat subjective, lets try it out and see if this kind of a commitment is measurable.

Mike: I see you give yourself one day not to tell her you love her..

Mike: That's in case I forget. I want to be able to be successful and reach my goals this week and not pay $5.00.

Mike: What do you mean by mail her a funny note one time?

Me: Oh, just tell her a joke or make up something silly and mail it to her, probably at work. Try to get her to smile particularly if she gets this during a stressful day. Sometimes I like to hide little notes in her lunch, she likes that.

Mike: You have to commit to me to be held accountable to do something like that?

Me: That's to make sure that I don't get too busy, or just not feel like doing it and let the week slip away.

In this example, I have gone from the vague "Improve

my relationship with Gail" to the specific, as illustrated in Figure 27.

Continuing with the steps, I would draw a mind map of what might stop me from performing these actions (Figure 28).

This is an opportunity for me to be brutally honest with myself. It is not easy to admit that I am selfish and might not care about what the relationship is going through. But high achievers, remember, are not in denial. They admit their limitations.

Based on the answers given in Figure 28, I have to ask myself whether I really want to improve my relationship. If so, I will need to either renegotiate my commitments (change them in some way) or change my attitude toward them.

Perhaps I would decide to commit to going out to dinner only once this week. I could still be human (not feel like going out, or be too tired, or be too busy) and still meet my commitment. This is renegotiating. I acknowledge my feelings and circumstances and renegoiate.

I could also write down the following statements to record on my reinforcement tape:

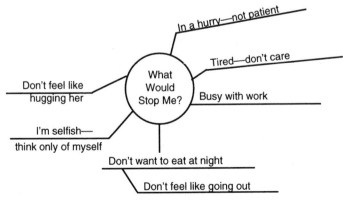

Figure 28

1. I am patient.
2. I have great energy all the time.
3. I care about Gail and everything she does and says.
4. I think of others all the time.

I have been using this partnering system since about 1985. I have gone through many partners. (It is time to change partners when it no longer matters if you did what you said you would do, you are missing your calls and not paying your fines.) I have had the same partner, Mike Grumet, a financial consultant with New York Life, for more than three years.

Mike has become a good friend and has been tremendously helpful to me in keeping me focused and on purpose. Remember, there is always the everyday struggle between The Alien and your good intentions.

I usually call Mike every Sunday night at about 8:45 p.m. I like to be done with our commitments and watch the 9 o'clock movie. Many times I might be on the road, traveling on Sunday, or just not feel like or be ready to give Mike my goals on Sunday. If that is the case, I have until Tuesday night to phone him with my commitments for the next seven days.

Rule Two has had to be enforced two times—once for me and once for Mike. "Recently, he didn't get his goals to me by two days from due date. There it is: an automatic $20.00 fine or he is no longer my support partner. It would have been easy for me to say, "That's okay. I know how busy you are. Let's really get focused for next week." That would have been incredibly selfish on my part, making myself feel better rather than confronting him and holding him accountable to his commitment.

My commitment to his success makes me hold him to his intentions for this week, and his commitment to my success makes him hold me to my intentions. As I sit at my computer on Friday at 10:30 p.m. putting these ideas on paper, I am being driven by my commitment to Mike that I would work on this book 10 hours this week. I plan on working Saturday, as well, but I really needed some hours tonight to make my 10-hour commitment. Because I know I am being held accountable to do a specific activity, it changes what paradigms I see. I see opportunities to perform, rather than reasons why I can't.

WHEN I HOLD MY PARTNER ACCOUNT-ABLE I AM GIVING HIM OR HER A GIFT

This morning I altered my behavior because of this part-nering system. I've done three of the four workouts (weight lifting and bike riding) to which I committed this week. But as of this morning I've yet to make all of the 200 prospect-ing phone calls to which I'm also committed. I'm 53 short. These prospecting phone calls are more important to me than the workout because Mike and I have a standing agreement in addition to the regular fines for not perform-ing my commitments. If I do not make those calls, I have to make an investment with Mike that I do not want to make at this time.

Mike has a similar "side bet." He has given a $100 check, made out to a competitor, to his manager. If he doesn't come through on a certain commitment, the manager has orders to mail the check.

Because of all this, I altered my usual morning schedule. I needed the time to make my 53 calls. I only did half of my workout—lifting weights—instead of lifting and then riding the bike, and I didn't go out for breakfast and read for 20 minutes. With this change in routine, I could get back to my office by 7 a.m., which is 10 a.m. East Coast time. Oth-

erwise, I would not have gotten to my office until about
8:30 a.m. California time. That is almost lunchtime on the
East Coast—too much time lost. I can always go back to
the gym after business hours and finish my workout.

Without stated goal-achieving activities and someone to
hold me accountable for them, I would not have been so
committed to performing those activities. I would have listened to The Alien. I would have slept in late, rationalized
(I need my sleep for energy), gone to breakfast, rationalized
(I need a good breakfast for health), got to the office late,
rationalized (I've still got time for *some* calls), and not made
all the calls I could have made, and rationalized again (I
was just too busy!).

As you become involved with this system, you might find
it takes a bit of trial and error to realize how much you really can commit to do within a seven-day period. Stick with
it! If you fall short, pay your fines and make more realistic
commitments for the next week. I totally disagree with the
old advice to shoot for more than you really want, the idea
being that if you fail you'll at least have more accomplished
than if you had made a lower commitment. This is a sure
way to sabotage your becoming a high achiever. It is better
to make realistic commitments. You will get better and better at meeting your commitments as time goes on. When
and if you do fall short, don't dwell on it. Pay your fine,
learn something, and move on.

You might learn, for example, that you really were not
committed to reach a certain goal. My friend Paul Krasnav-
age, a Rutgers football teammate and college roommate,
made a commitment for several weeks to lose 10 pounds.
He kept paying a fine and not reaching the goal week after
week. Finally he questioned his motivation and decided to
make a choice of either to remove the weight loss as a commitment or to actually do it. He choose to lose the weight
and off it came.

You will quickly grow tired of paying fines. This will enable you to learn the difference between a want or a "would like to some day" and a decision and commitment. A decision is *now*. A "some day" is in the future and does not compel performance.

Remember that with this system, *you* are the one who makes the commitments for yourself. Your partner does not make your commitments for you. Your partner is there to hold you accountable for what *you* say you are going to do. With this system, you won't be forced to do something you don't want to do. You are the one who makes the choices.

The great beauty of this system is that you give permission to someone else to hold you accountable for your *actions*. Actions, not promises, create results. Gene Murphy, the head football coach at Cal State Fullerton when I was there stressed this to our athletes every day.

He would tell them not to talk about their desire to win a championship but to take actions to guarantee it. That meant coming back in shape after the summer. That meant going to class and studying. That meant working out in the off season, and on and on. Our philosophy became: If we do the best we can, the winning will take care of itself. And it worked! We won championships when everyone else bet we were going to be at the bottom of the list.

I still live by this philosophy. Instead of committing to a certain number of bookings, I commit to a certain number of calls and new contacts. If I do what is necessary and I do it to the best of my ability, the results will take care of themselves.

Miscellaneous Notes about Partnering

I love the idea of $5 fines. There is no research that indicates $5 is better than any other amount. I like that amount because it causes you to be in control and to make choices. It creates an opportunity for you to exercise conscious control. You can choose to not do a certain activity and owe your partner $5 or you can choose to do it and keep the $5.

Mail cash to your support partner. Do not offset fines with one another. If you owe $10 and he owes $5, don't send just $5. You send the entire $10 and he sends the entire $5. You have to feel the loss.

You can meet in person, rather than over the phone, and you can have groups if you like. I don't advocate groups, because they are more difficult to keep together. There are different levels of motivation among the members. The advantages that you get from additional creative minds are offset because it takes longer and because of the differing levels of motivation.

Whether your meetings are over the phone or in person, keep them quick. You don't want the partnering part of this system to become a burden and seen as just another meeting you have to have. If it becomes a burden, it will be doomed.

You have enough information about the partnering aspect to be successful with it and to begin today. You can make up your own rules as well. Remember, our motto is: Whatever works and successfully competes with rationalization is acceptable. Please write me if you come up with any creative ideas about partnering.

Internal Support

You'll remember how the loan sales reps at that San Diego loan company didn't prospect, even though they said they were going to prospect, because of their true unconscious attitude toward prospecting. For them to feel like prospecting, they would have to change their attitude toward prospecting.

How do you change an attitude? Basically, you program your subconscious mind to believe that the *opposite* of the attitude is true. And that is what the internal support part of this system is all about.

By making a mind map of what would stop you from performing your goal-achieving activities, you've taken the first step in changing some of your attitudes.

The statement I wrote for my weight loss goal, "When I am hungry, I eat all the fruits and vegetables that I want," is an example. When I began my weight-loss program, I knew I would get hungry, and I also knew I should meet that hunger with fruits and vegetables rather than with cookies and cakes and pies. I *knew* this, but I really didn't *believe* it. For one thing, I didn't really like fruits and vegetables. If left to myself, without the aid of internal support, I would have met hunger by eating anything I wanted to eat *except* fruits and vegetables. So I wrote a statement that, when imbedded in my subconscious mind, would drive me to eating fruits and vegetables when I became hungry.

Whatever else may be correct or incorrect about the theories of behavioral psychologists, one thing is certain: We live in a stimulus-response world. (Does the name Pavlov ring a bell?) In my statement, "When I am hungry" is a stimulus; "I eat all the fruits and vegetables I want" is a response. To change an attitude, you must change your response to certain stimuli. The mechanics of how this works is best understood when the working of the brain is examined.

I'm not going to get into a deep scientific discussion here. Rather, I'm going to keep it simple and stick with the basics of the conscious (left) brain and the subconscious (right) brain, as discovered by Roger Sperry, a researcher at Cal Tech who won the Nobel Prize in 1982 for his left brain-right brain research. I was fortunate enough to study Sperry's work while I was at Cal Tech in 1979 (talk about being in the right place at the right time!).

The Nature of Consciousness

What is consciousness? Many people think you are conscious when you are "aware." Is "awareness" consciousness?

Awareness is not even necessary for learning. Here's a classic example. It's called "The Wandering Professor." There was a professor for an advanced psychology class who would stand at one side of the blackboard and lecture for a while, then wander across to the other side and continue his lecture, then wander back to the other side. Back and forth, back and forth, back and forth. It was very disturbing to the students.

They decided to teach him to stay at one side of the board for the entire class period. The way they would do it would be through his subconscious.

Every time he was at the side of the board they wanted him to be at, they looked directly at him with good eye contact. They smiled. They asked questions. They took notes. They thought positive thoughts.

Every time he wandered to the other side of the board, they wouldn't look at him. They did not ask questions. They did not take notes. They thought negative thoughts.

Before long, the professor spent entire class periods at the side of the board where the students wanted him to be. In fact, if he unconsciously started to wander as in the old days, he would stop and go back to the "preferred" side of the board.

Without his knowledge, without him being aware of it, he had been taught a behavior.

Most people think the answer is to be aware. When we sleep, we toss and turn hundreds of times during the night. We roll over to the edge of the bed but we do not end up on the floor. Why? We are aware that one more toss will put us on the floor. We are aware, but not awake.

Some people will suggest, then, that consciousness is the state of being awake, rather than being aware. Are you awake when you drive your car? I hope so. But how often are you conscious of what you are doing while you drive? Have you ever been at a stop light and a car pulls alongside and the occupants ask how to get to such-and-such a place? You say, "I'm going right by there on my way home. Follow me and I'll wave when you should make the turn."

The light turns green, you start off, and the grateful tourists are following you. Before you know it, you're pulling into your driveway, pressing the remote control for the garage door. You look in your mirror. Guess who's there? You forgot all about them. You were awake, but were you conscious?

The Conscious Mind

Research into the human brain has revealed that the conscious (left) brain has two important functions that relate to human achievement: reality testing (censoring) and inhibiting.

**THE FUNCTIONS OF THE CONSCIOUS MIND:
REALITY TESTING (CENSORING)
AND INHIBITING**

Part of the job of the left brain is to recognize danger so we can avoid it. It also filters out, through selective perception, things that are going on around us that are not dangerous so we can pay attention to other things that might be.

We discussed selective perception, as it applies to rationalization, earlier; and how it can have positive and negative effects on our behavior.

A common type of filtering done by the conscious mind

is that of noise. For example, if you were to move into a house near an airport, you would initially hear every plane that passed over your house. Soon, however, your conscious mind would realize the planes pose no threat to your survival, and you won't notice them. It will cause what is known as a *negative hallucination*; that is, you don't sense what is really there (rather than sensing something that is *not* there, as in a regular hallucination).

When my daughter Danielle was about one month old, I took a nap with her on my bed, falling asleep to the sound of the television. I was exhausted and slept deeply. The sound of the television made no impression on me. But, suddenly, Danielle started to hiccough and I was instantly wide awake and concerned. What was wrong? Was she choking on the milk she just drank? This is a classic example of filtering out what is not important while being instantly aware of something that is important.

The inhibiting function of the conscious mind is necessary for survival, too. We would not be able to function in our everyday lives without it. You would not be able to read the words on this page if you didn't have the ability to inhibit your mind from wandering. You are inhibiting right now as you are thinking about these concepts and not about what you are going to do tonight or what you are going to have for dinner.

You would not be able to cross the street in front of an oncoming truck without the conscious mind's ability to test reality (is that truck far enough away?) and inhibiting (I'd better stay on the curb). Without the conscious mind, you would step out into traffic and have that run-down feeling every day.

The inhibiting function of the conscious mind protects us in many ways. It came to my rescue at a gym where I was working out on a Stairmaster. A woman came in and started working out beside me. As she did so, she was fanning

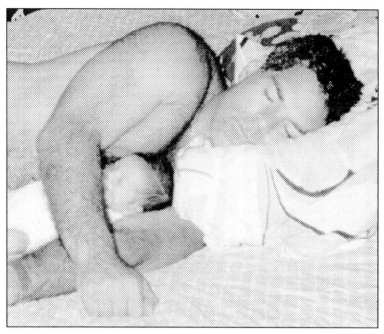

You might sleep through the noise of a blasting television in the room, but if your little daughter makes the slightest whimper, you'll instantly be wide awake.

Figure 29

herself with a small, handheld fan. The fan disturbed me. First, it was creating a cool draft I didn't like. Second, just the idea bothered me. I felt like reaching over, grabbing the fan, and throwing it onto the floor. I wanted to scream at her, "What's wrong with you? You're supposed to sweat! You are working out! And you are driving me crazy!"

Fortunately, the left side of my brain had a conversation with me. For once, The Alien came to my rescue. It said, "Don't do it, Bob. Just relax. She isn't bothering you. She has the right to use the fan no matter how ridiculous you think it is. Besides, you'd probably miss when you try to swat the thing out of her hand, hit her, get arrested for assault and battery, and go to jail."

That was inhibition and censoring at its best. Thank you,

conscious mind.

An important point to remember about the inhibiting function of the conscious mind is that it is largely *learned*. Children don't have it to the degree adults do.

When my daughter was three, I took her to a video store to buy a videotape for her. We walked by a candy counter and she demanded some. I said, "No." She immediately threw a tantrum, sprawling face-down on the floor, kicking her legs, screaming, "I want the candy!"

Can you imagine doing this as an adult? You do a great presentation for a client, ask for the business, and they say, "No." You throw yourself on the floor, kick your legs, and scream, "How can you say 'No'? What do you mean, 'No'? I've worked hard on this sale . . . !"

Unfortunately, as we grow up the conscious mind is also picking up inhibiting information from ourselves, our parents, our teachers, and our friends that is not necessary for survival and that keeps us from high achievement as adults.

As a demonstration of this in my workshops, I ask a person to stand on his or her chair. I tell them they are a famous singer and actor or actress for little children. They are to put their hand and their head, twirl around, and sing "Mary Had a Little Lamb" in a funny high voice.

Most people are willing to stand on the chair. Then the Alien gets a firm grip on them. The inhibiting conscious mind tells them, "Am I crazy? This is stupid! How is doing this going to help me be more successful. I look ridiculous. Some of these people know me, and this is embarrassing." It often takes a lot of coaxing on my part before they will twirl and sing.

This gives me the opportunity to explain how the conscious, inhibiting mind gets in the way of high achievement.

1. The activity is neutral. Twirling on a chair and singing a song is not, in itself, dangerous.

2. It is the perception of the activity, not the activity itself, that creates unwanted anxiety.

Going back to my first point about human nature getting
in the way of high achievement: How we think affects the
way we feel, which affects the way we act. In this case, it's
like Figure 30.

A person in this situation has two options:

1. Stop thinking about it. Just do it.
2. Think thoughts that support the activity.

```
STOP THINKING!
JUST DO!
```

If you don't think and just do, there is nothing to create
the anxiety. I use this in combination with the second option every time the alarm clock goes off at 5 a.m. and it's
time to get up and go to the gym. My left brain "reality
tests": I am tired, I was up until midnight, I'll be tired all
day if I don't sleep in. My subconscious (right) brain has
linked getting up early to pain and deprivation. Everything
is compelling me to stay in bed and rationalize.

Using Option One, when the alarm goes off I say to myself, "No thinking!" The Alien tries to talk to me. I say,
again, "Stop! No thinking! Just do!" Then I add something
like, "I love getting up early and working out." The Alien
interrupts, "That's a—." But I interrupt The Alien and say
to myself, "Stop thinking! Just do!" before The Alien can
finish, "a lie."

Using Option Two, I also think of things that support
getting up early and working out: "If I work out this morning, I'll be back in the office earlier. I won't need to go to

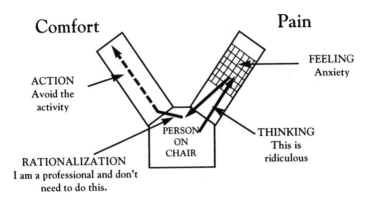

Figure 30

the gym in the evening. I'll feel better about myself and have a better day."

The same thing happens every day in each of our lives. You say your are going to work on a project or make a prospecting call or whatever. The Alien immediately jumps on your face, gets a firm grip, and tells you why you shouldn't do it.

Don't think! Just do!

Do all of your thinking *before* you make your commitment to an activity. After you make your commitment, just do!

In another demonstration of unnecessary inhibition, I ask the audience to participate in an oral fill-in-the-blank exercise. I say, "I want you to agree to do the following. When I say 'The subconscious mind accepts as being . . .' I want you to shout out the word 'true' as loudly as you can. Then when I say, 'Whatever is . . .' I want you to shout out 'vividly imagined.'

"How many of you are willing to do this?"

Usually, most of the hands go up. After a bit of discussion, I usually have everyone willing to participate. Then I have them put their right hand firmly on their face.

"That is The Alien," I tell them. "Now take it off and talk to your Alien. Thank it for caring and damn it for sharing. Now ... ready? The subconscious mind accepts as being ... whatever is . . . ."

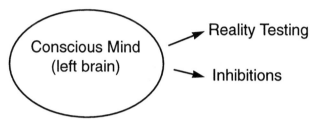

Figure 31

Out of 100 people who have committed to shout out "true" and "vividly imagined," only about 10 do it without inhibition.

What's going on here? They have all just committed to doing something. They gave their word. They pulled The Alien from their faces. What happened? The Alien sprang right back on. The Alien is more compelling. Avoiding pain—the possibility of being embarrassed—is stronger than the desire to take action and achieve.

> THE KEY IS TO USE THE
> INHIBITING POWER OF THE CONSCIOUS
> MIND TO INHIBIT THOUGHTS THAT TRY
> TO STOP YOU

The Subconscious Mind

The subconscious (right) mind is the part of the brain that is creative, intuitive, artistic, musical, imaging, and is activated when you are engaged in those types of activities.

That is what is so beautiful about mind mapping. It takes a left brain analytical activity such as planning and gives it the right brain touch, which opens up your creativity.

The most important thing to remember about the subconscious mind is this:

> **THE SUBCONSCIOUS MIND**
> **ACCEPTS AS BEING TRUE**
> **WHATEVER IS VIVIDLY IMAGINED**
> **OR SUGGESTED**

Because of this principle, we can program our minds to create the results we desire.

One of the best ways to illustrate this is with hypnosis. Hypnosis is an artificially induced state of extreme suggestibility. Hypnotic subjects suspend their usual critical, reality-testing apparatus and go along with the suggestions of the hypnotist. They respond to suggestion with their right brain, which accepts as being true whatever is vividly imagined or suggested.

I started the study of hypnosis in 1971 and became a hypnotherapist in 1980. When I was a coach, I gave hypnosis demonstrations to supplement my income and to nurture my passion for studying the mind.

My "show" was part of freshman orientation every year at Chapman College in Orange County, Calif. I would hypnotize several volunteers, then tell them that every time I clapped my hands, their chairs would be on fire. When I clapped my hands they jumped up, sure their chairs were on fire. The audience, of course, found this hilarious.

I would say to an individual, "You can't say your name. Every time I ask you your name, you stutter terribly. What is your name?"

"D-d-d-d-d-ave."

"When I touch you on the forehead, you can say your name clearly. What is your name?"

"D-d-d-d-ave."

I touch him on the forehead. "What is your name?"

"Dave."

At another show, I hypnotized an obese woman and told her she was a great singer and dancer, that she was famous and was here to perform. I told her that on the count of three she would sing and dance and flirt all over the room and among the audience. As soon as I said "three," she grabbed the microphone from my hand.

She sang. She danced. She flirted.

She had a beautiful voice that sounded as though she had had years of training. She danced wonderfully. When she was done, the audience gave her a standing ovation.

I told her, then, that I would count to three again and that she would remember everything she had just done. When I counted to three, she came back to "consciousness," and was one of the most embarrassed people I've ever seen. The electrical activity went from her accepting right brain to her critical left brain (conscious), where her internal dialogue (The Alien) was "I can't sing, I can't dance, I'm not attractive, they're not going to like me, I'm going to look foolish if I try to sing and dance."

Some years ago, the Russians conducted a similar experiment that shows my experience along these lines is not unique. Three people were hypnotized and told they were great artists. Then they were told to use the easels and paints and canvases in the room to paint portraits. None of these people were artists. None of them had training in art or painting. Yet, while hypnotized they created portraits as good, or better, than those of a professional artist. Their accomplishments under hypnosis, like the obese woman who sang, when the reality-testing, limiting left brain was not influencing their behavior, were far outside their belief system. What could *you* do if you transcended the boundaries of your belief system?

The soil of your mind will grow all kinds of seeds, good or bad. Every thought is a cause; every cause is an effect. Take control: Bring forth only desirable conditions.

> **ALL OF YOUR EXPERIENCES, EVENTS, CONDITIONS, AND ACTS ARE THE REACTIONS OF YOUR SUBCONSCIOUS MIND TO YOUR THOUGHTS**

In his book *The Power of the Subconscious Mind*, Dr. Joseph Murphy makes some very revealing statements:

> The subconscious mind has an infinite power and intelligence. It has the capacity to heal all conditions. Faith, as mentioned in the Bible, means a knowledge of the interaction of the conscious and the subconscious mind.
>
> The interaction of your conscious and subconscious mind requires a similar interaction between the corresponding system of nerves. The cerebrospinal system is the organ of the conscious mind and the sympathetic system is the organ of the subconscious mind. The cerebrospinal system is the channel through which you receive conscious perception by means of your five physical senses and exercise control over the movement of your

body. This system has its nerves in the brain and is the channel of your volitional and conscious mental action.

The sympathetic system, sometimes referred to as the involuntary nervous system, has its center in a ganglionic mass at the back of the stomach known as the solar plexus. It is the channel of that mental action which unconsciously supports the vital function of the body.

Your conscious mind grasps an idea which induces a corresponding vibration in your voluntary system of nerves. This in turn causes a similar current to be generated in your involuntary system of nerves, thus handing the idea over to your subconscious mind.

Change your thoughts and you change your destiny. Once the subconscious mind accepts an idea it begins to execute it.

How to get the subconscious mind to work for you:

1. First realize that your subconscious mind is always working;
2. Keep your conscious mind busy with expectation of the best;
3. Remember, just as water takes the shape of whatever it flows through, the life principle in you flows through you according to the nature of your thoughts;

4. Claim that the healing presence in your subconscious is flowing through you as harmony, health, peace, joy and abundance;
5. Think of it as a living intelligence;
6. It is done unto you as you believe.

Mark 11:24—What things soever ye desire, when ye pray believe that ye receive them, and ye shall have them. Believe and accept as true the fact that our desire has already been accomplished and fulfilled, that it is already completed, and that its realization will follow as a thing of the future. Faith is like a seed planted in the ground; it grows after is kind. Plant the idea (seed) in your mind, water and fertilize it with expectancy, and it will manifest.

Your subconscious mind magnifies the thoughts you deposit. You are here to grow, expand and unfold spiritually, mentally and materially. You have the unalienable right to fully develop and express yourself along all lines. You should surround yourself with beauty and luxury. Use your subconscious mind as a partner in success. Remember, what you are seeking is also seeking you. Nothing that happens to you is predetermined. The way you think, feel and believe determines your destiny.

The internal support part of my four-phase system helps you think, feel, and believe in ways that will alter your destiny to that of a high achiever. While the external support of your commitment list and your partner affects your conscious (left) brain, the internal support, which is a special kind of audiotape you will make, acts on your subconscious mind to uproot achievement-killing beliefs and replace them with achievement-making beliefs.

On your audiotape, you will put the statements you created earlier. Also on this tape will be selections of baroque music, which act as "keys" to open your subconscious mind so your statements are easily planted in it.

There is good, research-supported reasons for using baroque music in this way. The rhythm of energy is a part of all nature and human activity, including such involuntary actions as heartbeat, respiration, and brain waves. Some scientists have theorized that the rhythm of music can be linked to fundamental patterns of human growth, of physical and mental development, even to our survival.

Neurosurgeons studying Alzheimer's disease have discovered that repetition—especially with music—strengthens and creates *permanent* pathways of neural networks (Figure 32).

That means that when statements are repeated and reinforced, stimulus-response becomes *conditioned* stimulus-response.

A Swiss educator during the first part of the 20th century developed an educational system called Eurythmics for teaching children music. In this training, children are taught to create motor development and language development through a series of progressively complex musical patterns. He was convinced that memory, concentration, and coordination in adults depended on musical training in early childhood.

In an article titled "Sounding Out the Role of Music and Health," published in *Human Potential* magazine, the author writes that music is the "universe of chords." Further, she says, "Music seems to be a function of human evolution. No other lesser forms of life have evolved the capacity to create

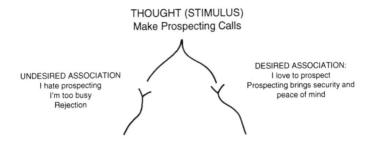

THOUGHT (STIMULUS)
Make Prospecting Calls

UNDESIRED ASSOCIATION
I hate prospecting
I'm too busy
Rejection

DESIRED ASSOCIATION:
I love to prospect
Prospecting brings security and
peace of mind

Through repetition, the desired pathway becomes
reinforced and eventually permanent while the
other pathway atrophies.

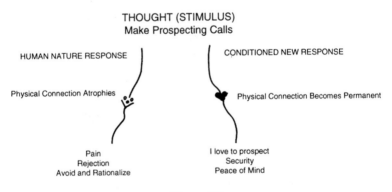

THOUGHT (STIMULUS)
Make Prospecting Calls

HUMAN NATURE RESPONSE

CONDITIONED NEW RESPONSE

Physical Connection Atrophies

Physical Connection Becomes Permanent

Pain
Rejection
Avoid and Rationalize

I love to prospect
Security
Peace of Mind

Figure 32

tones in a systematic manner or to store and recall those
tones as music. In fact, scientists are beginning to piece together ways music may advance our intelligence and en-
hance our capacity to learn. Throughout the ages, music
was prescribed as a medicine for afflictions of the digestive
tract, bones and joints, and for emotional disturbances. The

Greek scales were devised to bring about specific emotional states ranging from sleepiness to heightened passion."

Several years ago, Dorothy Retalack conducted some groundbreaking research with plants and music and published her findings in her book, *The Sound of Music in Plants*. She put various plants in different containers and played music in all of the containers except one. In that container was a "control group" of plants.

The plants that were entertained with rock-and-roll grew in contorted ways. Some shriveled and died. They all leaned away from the speaker of the sound system and from the wall (which naturally reverberated with the same rhythm as the music).

The plants that were regaled with classical music grew taller and thicker. They tended to lean toward the speaker by as much as 10 degrees.

Now she tried country-western music. What do you suppose happened? (I asked that question in a seminar once, and one of the participants said, "They cheated on their wives!" I don't ask that question in the seminar any more.) Actually, nothing happened. The plants that "listened" to country-western grew in the same way the control-group plants did.

The most intriguing of all was when she played baroque music. The plants exposed to this type of music used less water and fewer nutrients, and they grew taller and were healthier than any of the other groups of plants. They leaned toward the speaker by as much as 60 degrees.

She went further in her investigations. She theorized, as we did in Chapter 1, that "All matter is simply a form of energy: waves and pulsing vibrations." To find proof, she compared the energy, or vibrational states, of musical notes, colors, and elements.

In laboratory tests, she found that the note of G, with 192 vibrations per second, matches the energy vibrations of red and of iron. The note A, at 213 vibrations per second, matches the vibrations of red-orange and copper. The note B, at 240 vibrations per second, matches the vibrations of yellow and zinc.

Her conclusion from her research is sweeping and important: "We are finding that the universe is composed not of matter, but of music."

Another test that indicates the importance of music on human health was conducted not long ago at UCLA. There, researchers took a Kirlian photograph of a musician's finger before and while the musician played the third Brandenburg concerto. Before playing the music, the aura around the musician's finger was shaggy. While playing the music, the musician's finger became highly defined with beautiful, exciting lights.

Further corroboration of the relationship between living things and music has been offered by Susumu Ohno, a geneticist at the City of Hope Medical Center in Duarte, Calif., who was awarded the Emory Prize in 1981 for her work in reproductive genetics.

Ohno was struck by the flowing, repetitive nature of all genes in all creatures. They seemed to mirror the flow of music, so she devised a simple rule for converting genes to music. Although genes are complex chemical combinations, they are composed of only four basic types of nucleic acid: adenine, guanine, thymine, and cytosine. She assigned each of these acids two consecutive notes on the octave scale to create an eight-note scale.

When she translated genetic formulas to music using this method, Ohno found some amazing correspondences. The "music" of the gene that creates transparency in the lens of the eye is filled with airy and light trills and flourishes. A mouse gene sounds like a lively baroque waltz, even having striking similarities to Chopin's Nocturne, Opus 55, No. 1.

With these results, Ohno wondered what would happen

if she reversed the process and converted existing music to genetic formula. The conversion of Chopin's "Funeral March" was one of the most telling—and eerily appropriate. When converted to a genetic formula, entire passages of the composition are identical to a cancer gene found in humans.

Ohno concluded that art imitates life more than anyone ever expected, and went on to say, "What I think is at work here are underlying principles that govern many things: a gene, a bird's song, a classical composition. The same patterns that govern the movement of planets and galaxies also appear in genes and in music."

The effects of classical music on learning was demonstrated by researchers at the University of California at Irvine. Students listened to a tape suggesting that they imagine themselves relaxing in a garden, then took an IQ test. Then the same students listened to Mozart's Sonata for Two Pianos in D Major and took a similar test. Their scores averaged eight to nine points higher than before. One of the researchers said after the study, "We are testing a neurobiological model of brain function with these experiments, which proposes certain neural firing patterns in the brain. Listening to such music may stimulate neural pathways important to cognition."

The Importance of Baroque Music

The effects of baroque music on plants and its appearance in Ohno's research are especially intriguing when Lazonov's research into how people learn is taken into account. He found that when he played baroque music with a largo rhythm (60 beats per minute) for the schoolchildren he studied, they automatically went into the alpha state. More amazing yet, he found that children who were taught new material with this baroque music in the background learned an entire year's worth of information—without stress—in three months!

I learned about Lazonov's work and this seeming connection between human performance and baroque music while I was a coach at Cal State Fullerton. I was in a perfect position to put the theory to the test. I told my athletes that from now on we would listen to baroque music in the weight room, not the popular music we'd been playing.

They said, "You broke what?"

I explained it to them, and they all made a face. So we conducted our own experiment. I played some baroque music and had them hold their arms out. They were so strong, I could do chin-ups on their arms. Then I played popular rock-and-roll. They were as weak as a wet paper bag. They instantly became believers.

Using the power of baroque music as a foundation, I devised the four-step system explained in this book and applied it to our football team at Cal State Fullerton. We had nothing to lose by trying. We had been in the basement of the standings for so long, the team was acquiring a special taste for mushrooms. And the sports writers and odds makers were predicting we were going to eat mushrooms for some time to come.

Baroque music and the four-step system changed all that dramatically. That year and the next year we came in at Number One! We made no changes in the lineup, we made no changes in our training and drills. The only change we made was to use baroque music and this four-step system.

How Baroque Music Works for Goal Achievement

The idea that music can affect your body and mind certainly isn't new. For centuries, people have been singing lullabies to babies to put them to sleep. Singing while you work eases the labor and relaxes the mind. Music has the power to produce an "altered state" in your mind.

These altered states—when all the usual "laws" your conscious mind follows are suddenly suspended—have intrigued me for years.

We've all heard stories about a small woman who lifts an overturned car from the legs of her son so he can escape the wreckage, or of the woman who dashes into a burning house and carries a 300-pound man to safety.

What's going on here? In their normal waking state, they wouldn't be able to accomplish either feat. Ordinarily, the conscious mind would say, "You can't do that. The car's too heavy, the man's too heavy, you've never lifted anything like that before and you can't do it now." But in the altered state caused by emergency, they do it.

Have you ever been in a situation where you were sure you were going to die in the next moment? This happens frequently in automobile accidents or near-accidents.

I was talking about this one day to a friend of mine, who related his own story. He was driving on a divided highway in California, following a semi that was heavily loaded and traveling slowly. My friend started to pass the truck. As he did so, a truck traveling in the opposite direction, on the other side of the divided highway, lost a wheel. Not just a tire. The entire wheel.

The wheel rolled and bounced and crossed the median and came right at my friend's car. He couldn't go to the right. The truck he was passing was in the way. He swerved to the left, onto the shoulder, and the wheel just missed him.

The interesting thing about the whole incident, he said, was that it all happened so slowly, as though the universe suspended all laws of time and motion to give him the time to make just the right evasive maneuver.

It wasn't until it was all over that the adrenaline reaction hit him. He shook so much he had to pull over to the side of the road until he calmed down.

This "slowing down" of time is common in such "near

death" experiences. The universe doesn't really slow time down. Your mind does. It is an altered state. The delayed reaction of shock is also common.

I had a similar experience of my own when I was 17 and a rookie life guard at a New Jersey beach. Part of our training was working with a rowboat. It was a huge wooden rowboat pointed at both ends. And it was dangerous. If we ever used it to rescue someone, we'd probably hit them with the boat and kill them. But we used it in training anyway.

I had always been told that if a wave is about to break over the boat to be sure the boat was facing into the wave. That way, the wave would just break over the boat. It might fill it with water, but it wouldn't capsize.

One day I was in the boat, facing the shore. I looked over my shoulder to see a huge wave coming at the boat. Now, I wasn't thinking clearly. I should have kept the boat as it was. The stern was just as pointed as the bow, and the wave would have broken over the boat harmlessly. But I was thinking, "Face the wave!" I started to turn the boat with the oars, and timed it just right for disaster.

The next thing I knew, I was under the boat, and under the water. Amazingly, rather than fear, I had a great feeling of peace. I pushed the boat over and came to the surface. The whole incident couldn't have taken more than a few seconds, but it seemed like hours. When I got back to the beach, I started trembling. I was horrified at what almost happened.

After I related this story during one of my seminars, a woman who was a flight attendant told a similar story. On one of her flights, the plane went through a flock of geese during takeoff. The two right engines caught fire and the pilot had to make an emergency landing.

This woman went through all the emergency procedures she had been trained to do. One of the passengers, a huge man weighing at least 250 pounds, panicked. He was standing up, holding the seatback in front of him in a death grip. With superhuman strength, she pulled him into his seat and buckled him in.

When she was through with her duties, she went to her own seat and fastened her seat belt. Only then did she succumb to terror. She trembled and shook with fear.

In telling her story, she recalled that for her, too, time was distorted while she performed her tasks. There was no fear until the tasks were done.

These "near death" experiences are altered states. You are conscious, but in a different way from "normal" consciousness. Every day of our lives, we are in and out of altered states every waking hour.

The Alpha State

Look away from this page and spell the word "geography." All right, now look away from this page again and spell "geography" backward.

Your eyes probably went up. If they did, you probably didn't see the ceiling. When performing an exercise such as spelling a word, most people's eyes go up in what is called a "non-visual eye movement pattern." You aren't seeing the wall or the ceiling.

If you are right-handed and your eyes moved up and to the left, you were "seeing" the word as though it were on a screen.

This is another type of altered state. It's the "alpha" state, and it's a state of mind that's very important for our purposes.

Lazonov discovered during his study of schoolchildren in Bulgaria that they learned best when in an alpha state. Their breathing is relaxed, they have a slower heartbeat.This state makes your mind more open to new data, and it helps you remember it better. He also discovered that the alpha state can be induced just by listening to music. Not any old kind of music, however, but a special kind of music that's been around for more than 200 years: baroque music.

Certain types of music—especially baroque music—can induce the same kind of alert, yet relaxed, state as certain types of meditation. Transcendental meditation, for example, has been shown to relieve inner tension, lower blood pressure, provide stress control, and improve physical and emotional health. Certain baroque music appears to do the same thing—with one big difference: You don't have to find a quiet place and close your eyes and chant a mantra.

Largo-movement baroque music, with its very slow bass that beats like a human pulse, will lower your heart rate to about 60 beats per minute. Your blood pressure drops. Your alpha waves increase. It's automatic. You don't have to tell your body to relax.

When you are in this relaxed but alert state with increased alpha-wave activity, your mind is in a receptive mode. And when you are in that receptive mode, you can reprogram your mind for achievement. We will use the benefit of music in our program to reinforce the state of mind necessary to create more effective performance.

The Concept of Modeling

Successful people are successful because they share certain patterns of thought and action that lead to success. If you want to be the best at anything, model yourself after the best.

The Russians take a young gymnast with great talent and put him into a sports camp where he spends all his time with world-class gymnasts. What does that person become? A world-class gymnast. Why? Because he takes on the behavioral characteristics of that model.

When I was in graduate school and a graduate assistant wrestling coach, Jeff Blatnick became a model for me, not just for excellence and high achievement, but for persistence and a sense of urgency and tenacity. He proved to be a model for our entire team, as well.

A model is someone who has created a strategy for success and proves that it works. All you have to do is duplicate that strategy. How do they rule their lives? What do they do to achieve the results you want to achieve?

While coaching football at Cal State Fullerton, I met another high achiever who is a business model. At the time, I lived in a cottage about a block from the beach in Corona del Mar. As a bachelor not making much money, the decor left a little to be desired. The curtain on my bedroom window was a blue sheet. My bookcases were made of cement blocks and boards. Old telephone cable spools were my end tables. An upside-down plastic milk crate was my coffee table.

About a year after I quit coaching and started giving my seminars, I was in better financial shape. One day I went home and looked around. "I can't live like this any more," I told myself. So I bought a three-bedroom, two-bath house in the prestigious Turtle Rock area of Irvine.

Now I had to furnish it. You can't put milk crates and cement blocks in a house like that.

I went to a furniture store just to look around and price things. I had no idea of what I wanted. I just wanted to look around.

When I went into the store, a salesperson came up to me. He introduced himself politely and asked, "May I help you?"

I looked him straight in the eye and said, "I'm not going to buy anything today. I just bought a new house, and I don't even know what I'm going to buy. I just saw your sign, I'm just looking around, this is the first store I've been in related to furniture and I'm not going to make a decision today."

Still polite, he said, "Well, I'm here if you need any help," and he went away.

As I wandered through the store, another salesperson came up to me. She introduced herself and asked, "Can I help you?"

I went through my litany again: "I'm not going to buy anything today, I just bought a new house, etc., etc."

She smiled and said, "Sure, I'll be around if you need any help."

I thought, "I've got it made, nobody's going to bother me today."

Then another salesperson came up to me. He shook my hand with too much pressure, he shook it too high, he shook it too low. He introduced himself and said, "How can I help you?"

I had my lines down pat. "I'm not going to buy anything today. I just bought a new house...."

He exclaimed, "A new house!"

"...and I don't know what I'm going to get...."

"A new house and you don't know what you're going to get! Tell you what..." He grabbed my arm "I have a background in interior design and decorating. Why don't we go over to your house right now and I'll help you out. No obligation. I'll give you some ideas of what kind of furniture might be great in your room. We'll measure it all out, we'll give you some ideas. You don't even have to buy from me and you certainly don't have to buy today. Does that sound like a fair deal?"

I said, "Well...."

Before I could finish my answer, he had me out the door and we each drove our own cars to my new house. He walked through the room with a clipboard in one hand and a tape measure in the other. He drew diagrams as though he was an architect building a new house, not just a furniture salesman figuring out furniture for it.

"Here," he said, putting the end of the tape measure in my hand. He made another measurement. "Oh, I've got a great idea for a couch here. It comes with a free—*free*—love seat. I hope we still have it in inventory."

In the bedroom he asked me about drapes. I said, thinking of my blue sheet, "Hey now, nothing expensive. I just need something to block out the sun!"

When it was all over, he said, "We've got some great deals for you, but they're only on sale while they're in inventory now, so let's hurry up back to the show room. We can get you the best deal possible!"

I said, "Wait a minute. You don't know who you are talking to. My name is Bob Davies and I do training for sales people. I know that you're creating a sense of urgency."

He said, "Yeah, I know. Let's hurry up and get back!"

We set land speed records getting back to the showroom. Once there, he took me by the arm and dragged me all around the store.

At a couch: "Sit down. How does this feel? It comes with a free—a *free*—love seat!" He showed me on the diagram exactly where it would go in my living room.

"Now, he said, we need an end table. We recommend oak. You like oak, don't you?"

I was ready to wring his neck. I thought, "Oh, no. Here he goes. He's doing a Tommy Hopkins trial close. I'm hip. I know what he's doing." So I said, "Yeah, I like oak."

Then he went too far. He said, "Which one of these do you like? This one or this one?" I felt like breaking the guy's neck. I said, "I like that one." And he smiled and said, "I like that one too."

I was ready to murder him. I was in resistance. I wasn't going to buy from him. But this guy would not stop.

"Now," he said, "we need some lamps for your end tables. I like brass. I recommend brass. You like brass, don't you?"

I almost yelled it: "Yes! I like brass!"

"Which one of these do you like best? This one or this one?"

I said, "That one!"

He pointed to the other one and said, "Do you like that one as well?"

I was shocked. I said, "Yeah I like that one as well, but I already said this one. Why are you asking me about that one?" I was ready to kill him.

He said, "Because it's fifty dollars less. I can get you a better deal on that one. It's just as nice, isn't it?"

Sure enough, it was just as nice and he saved me $50. Now, when he did all this, he had me on his side. He was my ally. From that point on, it was him and me against the furniture store. I bought everything that day, including $1,500 worth of drapes! (Which is a lot, going from a blue sheet). The only reason I bought those drapes is that he gave me a free $50 bedspread that had a color that matched those $1,500 drapes. I don't know about you, but I just can't pass up a bargain.

A few days later, when the furniture was delivered, he came to my house to make sure everything was in place just the way I wanted it. Then he added, "You know, we have another sale coming up. Do you know of any people I can talk to about coming down and buying from me?"

I said, "Well, not really."

My subconscious mind was really saying, "I don't feel like doing it. I don't care enough about you to sit down and find referrals for you."

However, I didn't say that. I said, "I'll think about it and I'll let you know."

He said, "Could you think about it right now? You have a Rolodex right here on your table. Would you mind, since I'm here, going through the Rolodex and see if any names pop up that I might contact?"

I gave him about five names. I don't know how he did,

but I'm sure he got someone to come down to that store and buy some furniture.

Here's the point of the story: The first two salespeople who approached me at the furniture store should follow that guy around for a few days and see what he does. Then they should do the same thing. He made the sale. They didn't.

First of all, the first two salespeople asked *whether* they could help me. The guy who sold the furniture to me asked, "*How* can I help you?" There's an assumption there. He is assuming he is going to help me. He just wants to know how. The other two were asking for permission.

He fought through my resistance like a hot knife through butter. He got what he wanted, which was the commission. I got what I wanted, which was a house filled with furniture. I didn't really want to just look around. I just wanted to get a good deal. I didn't want to go down the street and see the same things for $500 less. He took care of me and his service was spectacular.

He was consistent, persistent, a self-starter, a great communicator. He came across with great personal confidence. He built rapport and trust (rapport built by the lamp, saving me $50). He was creative (he followed me to my house and had me participate). He did follow-up and asked for referrals. He was assertive, aggressive. He had the belief that I wanted to own some furniture so he was going to be the one to sell it to me. He was friendly. He had empathy. He assumed the sale. He was tactful. He matched my style (I went back to the store one day and saw him hunched over, speaking very slowly, walking very slowly, showing an elderly couple some furniture. When he was finished, he sprinted over to me and shook my hand and said, "Don't you just love your new furniture?").

Whatever your goals are, it's a good idea for you to find someone who is already successful at achieving those goals.

Find out what they do that makes them successful and make a mind map of it. Then use that mind map for your own goal achievement.

In Appendix A is a mind map of a successful sales personality profile, along with the statements that reinforce the beliefs of a successful salesperson. This profile was compiled after interviews with many successful salespeople in a variety of fields. You'll see how this furniture salesman fits the profile exactly.

How To Record Your Reinforcement Tape

When you created your mind maps of what you want, of the activities you need to perform to get what you want, and of what might stop you, you also created statements, or "scripts," that you want to plant in your subconscious mind. Gather those statements together.

Now go through the sample scripts provided in Appendix B and add any that are appropriate to you.

You will need two tape recorders. Load into one a tape of baroque music (see the order form at the back of this book for a taped collection of baroque music to use). Load into the other a blank tape. Have your scripts in front of you, ready to read.

Hold one tape recorder in one hand and the other in the other hand. Turn the baroque-music recorder to "play," and the blank-tape recorder to "record." Play the baroque music loudly enough so you can hear it, but not so loudly that it drowns out your voice. Hold both players about three inches from your chin.

Read each of your statements you have at least six times, three times in the first person (I) and three times in the second person (you). For example, "I respond to rejection with enthusiasm and dollar-producing activities. You respond to rejection with enthusiasm and dollar-producing activities"

Use a strong, authoritative, commanding voice. Remember: You are ordering your subconscious mind to obey and respond.

Play with the beat to the music. Be creative. There is no right or wrong way to record. Notice the four-beat tempo to baroque music. Slow-moving, largo tempo has 60 beats per minute. Be creative. Change the volume of your voice, the tempo, the pace. Make this a masterpiece.

Once you have recorded your tape you will have space left. Here are some recommendations. First, think about habits that you might want to create and record them. Suggestions:

I contact my support partner every week.
I get gas in my car when it is on half.
I am on time with my Daytimer.
My desk is neat and clean.
My car is neat and clean.

Identify attitudes and activities that you will always want to have or do in your business. If you are in sales and will always need to do a certain prospecting activity, then put that on your tape. Wherever you can identify a weakness in your personality, put statements that make it a strength on your tape.

Have fun with this. Take it seriously. Keep it confidential and keep the tape in your car. Listen to your tape as much as you want to. I recommend at least four times per week, at least five minutes per session. You don't have to consciously pay attention to the content of your tape. Just play it. The music will create the altered state and give you direct access to the keyboard of your brain, the subconscious mind.

Conclusion

Now you have the secret of high achievement and peace of mind (Figure 33).

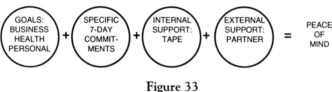

Figure 33

This is the structure of creating focus and accountability:

1. What do I want?
2. What do I need to do to get what I want?
3. What would stop me, what circumstances and attitudes?
4. Negotiate, change my plan and/or counter these attitudes by changing my thinking.
5. Create my seven day behavioral contract.
6. Commit to my support partner.
7. Listen to my reinforcement tape.

Select a strong and committed partner. Create specific measurable objectives for a 7-day plan. Pay your fines, recommit every week. Listen to your tape and be the best person you can be. Work with integrity and focus.

All of human nature is going to try to compel you to avoid doing what you committed to with your partner. The Alien will compete with you every day and try to get you to stop using this program. That is, unless you compete right back with "Stop thinking! Just do!" Every time you hear from your tape, "I do what I said I would do," your Alien loses its grip. You can compete successfully with human nature and win— and it is easy!

Before I end this book, I want to make one last point about a phenomenon of human nature. It is called *packing*.

Look at Figure 34. Note that the 2% at each end of the bell curve are labeled "abnormal." At the center, where most people are, is "normal." We are taught all of our lives to conform and be like other people. There is a tremendous pull from this "normal" part of the curve. High achievers are *not* normal! For you to stay with the elite high achievers, you have to constantly reinforce a point of view that steers you clear of the "normal." Low achievers stay at the low end by reinforcing reasons for non-performance, reasons that support "can't". High achievers stay at the high end by reinforcing reasons for performance, reasons that support *"can."* The moment either one of these extremes stops its reinforcement , the center pulls it like a magnet.

Remember that fear is a lie. Go out and prove it to yourself by doing something that your Alien says you can't do.

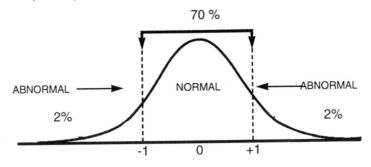

Figure 34

Confront your fear. Go jump out of an airplane or do a ropes course. Challenge yourself. Helen Keller said that life is either a great challenge or nothing at all!

You can use this four-phase strategy for any goal in any area of your life. Thousands of people who have attended my workshops live their lives according to it. They have learned to make deals with themselves and not feel deprived. They have learned how to plan and change their attitudes to support their intentions. Now you, too, have the secrets for doing this.

I hope you are committed to the challenge of self-actualization. I hope it matters that you are as good as you can be.

Please write to me and let me know what breakthroughs you have. I really do care about your successes.

GOD'S GIFT TO YOU
IS YOUR POTENTIAL.

YOUR GIFT TO GOD
IS WHAT YOU DO WITH IT.

Afterword

From the time we are born, we are programmed with beliefs that we accept as being true. Most of these mental programs are false. But, again, the subconscious mind doesn't distinguish between what is real and true and what is false, it just responds. The brain has long been compared to a computer. A computer does not have intentions, it simply carries out commands.

Because of my background I had many commands that were not working. I was the middle child in a poor family. For awhile I had an alcoholic stepfather. He eventually left, leaving my mother trying her best to cope with raising a family. We were at the poverty level, on public assistance, and times were rough.

I learned early that to "survive" I could depend on only myself. I learned to isolate myself from people, including my family. My family structure was completely out of control. Everyone did whatever they pleased. My brother and sister got involved with drugs.

I was luckier. I got involved with sports. The luck was that I had a coach who held me in higher esteem than I held myself. Because of my experiences with a coach and a healthy activity to focus on, I graduated high school, went on to college, and finally earned a masters degree in psychology. This is all the more amazing when you consider that I am the only one in my immediate family to have ever graduated high school . My mother, sister, and brother never made it through high school.

Another human being—a coach—taking an interest in your performance makes a big difference. So I am a success story. Poor boy done good.

But I had to overcome the commands in my subconscious about low self-worth. I had no idea of what love was. There was absolutely no love model in my household. Therefore, I was very poor in relationships. The only thing I had going for me was that I was driven and was willing to work hard.

I remember that my high school football coach told me when I was a junior that I was good enough to get a scholarship to college—me, a 6-foot, 170-pound linebacker! He also told me I would need to weigh at least 200 pounds to do it. So at a very critical time in my life I had a command in my subconscious mind: to survive I had to overeat. And that I did. I came back from summer vacation with an additional 35 pounds of muscle and fat. Sure enough, I made All State and was given a scholarship to play football and attend Rutgers University. A dream come true.

While at Rutgers I was surrounded by other All State star players and they were all bigger than I. I got up to 235 pounds one season, but couldn't hold that weight and played at 205. The firm command about my eating habits was well established.

At Rutgers, I learned some other subconscious lessons. These athletes were better than I. The only way to compete was to outwork them, to be more aggressive than they were, and to want it more.

That was my coping strategy. It worked as I went on to become a coach. My aggressiveness and work ethic fit right in. I had an eating problem, but I was able to control it by compensating with my workouts.

Then in 1983 I left coaching to conduct my seminars full-time. Now I was in for an eye-opener. I was in sales for a living, selling my consulting services. I was weakest at the greatest asset a successful salesperson has: creating relationships with people and having people like me and be on my side. I burned so many bridges with my aggressiveness and anger that today some of those bridges still come back to haunt me.

The only thing keeping me out of the poor house was my work ethic and my ability to stay out of denial. I knew I had a problem. Therapy was helpful, but not the answer. Finally, I discovered the baroque music technique of attitude enhancement. Now all I needed was a model.

I interviewed as many successful people as I could find who would talk to me. I talked with Tony Galie, a college roommate of mine who had become a very successful businessman. Everyone liked Tony. You got the feeling that he really cared about you when you were talking to him. I picked his brain. How to you react when someone rejects you? What do you think when someone lets you down? And so on. I interviewed another friend, Ed Laird—business owner, entrepreneur, and millionaire. How do you run your business? What do you think of . . . ? I interviewed successful people in my field, the speaking industry. From these interviews I developed a series of scripts that I would use to program into my mind.

I made a reinforcement tape. I put such statements as "I am a good person. I care about other people. I respond to others with their needs in mind first. I respond to rejection with love and vitality. Rejection gives me energy. I keep on keeping on."

I decided to create different eating habits, so I put statements such as "I chew my food slowly. I love salads. I crave salads." on my tape.

I put on the tape statements regarding business performance: "I do things now. I do what I said I would do."

This tape is very strong and private. I keep the tape in my tape player in my car at all times ,and listen to it at least four times a week, for at least five minutes a session. Usually

I listen to it much more than that. The more rejection I get, the more difficult the challenges become, the more I maintain mental stability and peace of mind by listening to my tape.

This four-phase system has helped me become much more successful than I could have become otherwise. It hasn't taken all the stress out of my life. Nothing can do that. But it has drastically altered my attitude toward the stressful things.

For example, I was sitting in my office one day reflecting on some very stressful things that were going on at that time. I was involved in an expensive wrongful-termination lawsuit filed by one of my ex-employees (who was actually an independent contractor). I was going through a divorce and my wife was trying to use my daughter as a wedge. I was having a difficult time with one of my promoters on the East Coast. I had an equity share in a house with a person who was living in the property and not paying the mortgage. I had just discovered my office manager had been forging checks.

As I was running all this through my mind, I leaned back in my chair and said to myself, "With all of this going on, why am I in a good mood? I feel great!" Then it dawned on me. For the past several years I had been hearing on my tape, "I am in a good mood all the time. Only good happens to me. I am a spiritual and mental magnet attracting good to myself."

These events certainly weren't all good. They were negative. But they would lead to great learning, lessons, and positive growth.

My own life proves that this system really works. With it I have been able to re-engineer my personality for greater happiness and success. If it works for me, it will work for *anyone*.

Appendix A
Sales Personality Profile & Script

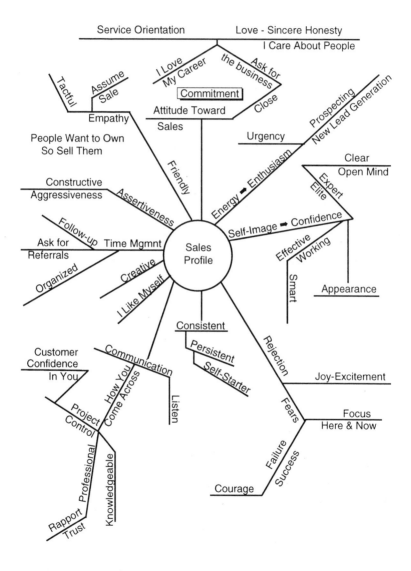

Figure A-1

I respond to rejection with enthusiasm and positive, dollar-producing activity. Rejection gives me energy. I respond with love and vitality. I keep on keeping on.

I have joy and excitement in my life at all times.

I deserve and I am extremely successful. I have a here-and-now focus all the time. I deserve success and prosperity and I am successful and prosperous.

I have great courage in everything I do. I am a risk taker. Risk taking is fun and I do take risks.

I am consistently a top performer. I am persistent. I am a self-starter. I am highly motivated.

I am a great communicator. I listen well to all people.

I have only constructive self-evaluation. I forgive myself for any errors and I always learn. Every situation is a positive and learning situation.

I am professional. I am always respected and perceived as being professional and classy.

I am extremely knowledgeable in all areas of my business.

I build tremendous trust and rapport with everyone I come into contact with. Everyone I deal with has trust and confidence in me. I am in control of all situations.

I am creative. I am creative. I am creative.

I am an expert at managing my time effectively and I do. I am great at follow-up. I always ask for referrals.

I am organized. I am organized. I am organized.

I am constructively assertive and aggressive all the time. I understand that people want to own, so I sell them. I am friendly all the time. I have empathy. I am tactful. I assume the sale. I am a great sales presenter and closer.

I love sales. I love sales. I love sales. I am a great closer. I am a great closer. I always as for the business. I love my career.

I am committed. I do what I said I would do on time or before. I live my life as my commitments. I make a plan and I do it because I said I would.

I am service oriented. The best thing I can do for the people I come into contact with is to get them happily involved with me today.

I treat other people with love. I am sincere. I respond to other people with their needs in mind first. I care about other people. I am honest.

I have tremendous energy and enthusiasm all the time.

I love to prospect and I do. Prospecting is fun and I do prospect. I am a great and expert prospector.

I am a great person and an expert in sales. I am extremely confident in everything I do. I am open minded. I have a sense of urgency and a do-it-now attitude.

I am a perpetual selling machine. I am a perpetual prospecting machine.

I am clear headed, refreshed and alert at all times. I look

and act professional and successful all the time.

I have reached my goals this month and every month. I reach my goals. I feel great all the time. I am a successful person. I am in a good mood all the time.

I am one with the infinite reaches of my subconscious mind. It is my right and I am happy, rich, and successful.

Money flows to me freely, endlessly, and copiously. I am forever conscious of my true worth.

I give of my talents freely and I am blessed financially and with good health.

Divine order takes charge of my life today and every day. All things work together for good for me today. There will never be another day like this one. This is a good and wonderful day for me.

I am divinely guided all day long. Whatever I do, I prosper. Divine love surrounds me, enfolds me, and enwraps me, and I go forward in peace.

I am a spiritual and mental magnet, attracting to me all things that are good, bless, and prosper me. I have attracted all things that are good, bless, and I am prosperous and healthy.

I have been a wonderful success in all of my undertakings today. I am definitely happy all day long.

Appendix B
Sample Scripts

PHYSICAL AND NUTRITION

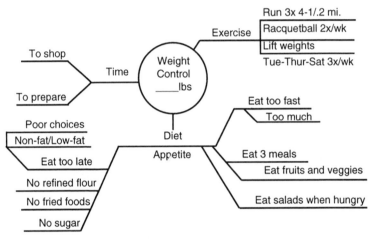

Figure B-1

I am loved, safe, secure, sexy and aroused as I weigh _____
pounds or less in _____. My stomach is hard and my
sides are slim and trim. I am in great shape as I weigh _____
pounds or less.

I thrive on exercise. Exercise makes me successful in all as-
pects of my life. As I love all people I do exercise.

I run at least _____ times per week for at least _____ miles
per run. I love to run and I do. I love the feeling in my legs
as I effortlessly run. It is beautiful and relaxing as I do run.

I play racquetball at least _____ times per week. Racquetball releases chemicals in my body that keep me healthy

and energetic. I am addicted to racquetball.

I lift weights every _____, _____ and
_____ of every week forever. I love the feeling of
being slim and trim and in great shape. I hear the compliments that people give me because I am slim, trim, and in
great shape.

Hunger is my friend. When I feel hungry I recognize that
this is my body's way of thanking me for keeping us healthy.
I eat only when I am hungry and only the amounts that I
need to stay completely healthy. I am completely healthy.

I eat only foods that are good for me. My subconscious
mind uses only the amounts of calories that I need to maintain perfect health and I am in perfect health.

When I am hungry, I eat all of the fruits and vegetables that
I want. Fruits and vegetables satisfy my hunger and taste
great. I feel full when I eat fruits and vegetables.

I am always on a diet. I take great pride as I have great control of my eating habits because I desire the feeling of being
slim, trim, and in great shape. I hear the compliments that
people give me because I am slim, trim, and in great shape.

I chew my food slowly, enjoying it thoroughly. I chew my
food slowly, less food tastes great. I am an efficient eating
machine. I am a lean, effective, healthy person.

I eat non-fat foods at all times. I eat only foods that are
good for my body.

I eat only up until 10 p.m. I take great pride in going to bed
hungry. As I hug _____ I love to go to bed hungry. As I

make money and have a successful career, I love to go to bed hungry. My purpose and challenge in life is to go to bed hungry in life and I do.

I take time to shop and prepare foods for myself. When I eat out, I eat salads and other low-fat and well-prepared foods.

I love to run and I do. Running is healthy for me. Running helps me to make a lot of money and I do run and make money. Running helps me to reach my goals and to love other people and I do run and reach my goals and love other people.

I love to get up early and I do. I take pride that I am doing something that most people won't do. I love the darkness as I run. I love the chill in the air.

My knees feel great all the time. I have a healthy blood flow in them and they work great. My entire body is healthy.

I exercise for life. I exercise for the rest of my life. I think only of today's workout. Here and now!

When I eat foods that have a taste I love, I find that I get filled up very quickly. I crave salads. I crave salads. I crave salads.

I am disciplined. I stay on my exercise and diet schedule.

Whenever I have a thought that does not support my workout and diet, I immediately destroy that thought. I have only positive thoughts that forward the action. If my thoughts don't help me, I stop thinking and just do.

I always have energy. I always have great workouts.

I sleep soundly all the time. I sleep soundly all the time. My body needs only _____ hours of sleep.

As I make money and reach my goals, I stay on my program.

INSURANCE SALES

Figure B-2

I am loved, safe, secure, as I have sold at least _____ policies in _____. As I love my family, I have sold at least _____ policies this month.

I love to prospect and I do. Prospecting is fun and I have made at least _____ calls per day, every day, Monday through Friday, this month.

I am an expert on the phone. I effectively use the phone and get results.

I have at least _____ appointments per day: _____ day appointments and _____ evening appointments. I have appointments six days a week.

I have a weekly mail program. This is automatic for me. Every week I mail out at least _____ pieces.

I love to canvass business and I do. I have spent at least two hours per day in the morning canvassing.

I get large numbers of quotes for group health insurance every day. I have at least _____ quotes to present in _____.

I have at least _____ people in my seminar at the end of _____.

I have sent mail regarding the seminar to present policy holders by the end of the second week of _____.

I get at least three referred leads from every sale.

I upgrade my existing policy holders and review their coverage two times every year.

AUTOMOBILE SALES

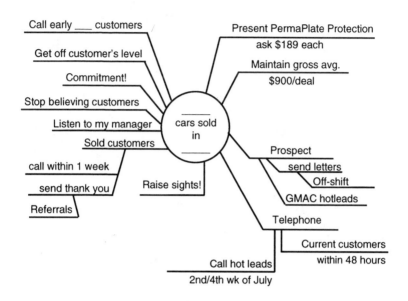

Figure B-3

I am loved, safe, secure, arouses, as I have sold _____ units in _____. As I love my family, I have sold _____ cars in _____.

I maintain a gross average of $_____ per deal earned to the company.

I have a great attitude toward prospecting. I love to prospect and I do. I take control of my ups. I create ups. I am an expert in the car sales business.

I have sent out _____ letters the first week of _____ to the hot leads. I have sent out _____ letters the third week of _____. I do this in my off-shift hours. I have pride as I control my own destiny.

I call current customers within 48 hours of meeting them. I stay in touch with the "be backs." I sell them their car.

I have called the hot leads the second and fourth weeks of _____. This is productive and leads to sales.

I am a worthy person. I deserve to earn $_____ and I do. I am a successful person. I have high expectations for myself.

I am very organized. I send out a thank-you note and a referral request to every sold customer.

I contact each sold customer within one week of the sale.

I am committed to this business. This is my career. I love this business and I am outstanding in the business. I am an expert.

I maintain a highly professional and successful manner all the time. I am successful.

I make _____ calls per day _____ times per week to last year's customers.

I am responsive to training. I listen to my manager. I sell the customer.

I present the (warranty name) to all sold customers. I ask for $_____ each.

LOAN ORIGINATORS

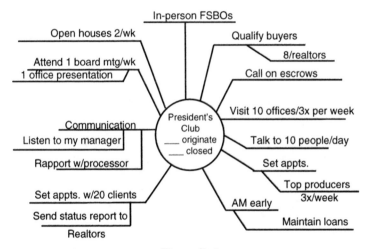

Figure B-4

I am proud, loved, safe, and secure, as I have originated _____ loans and funded _____ in _____.

I have visited at least _____ three days per week every week of _____. As I love _____ I do go into offices.

I talk to at least _____ people every day.

I set appointments with top producers. I am a great loan originator. I create great rapport with everyone. I set appointments with _____ top producers every week.

I go into the office early and maintain my loans.

I have set at least _____ appointments with clients.

I stay in contact with real estate brokers. I send status letters in a timely fashion.

I answer my pager and stay up to date on my messages and return calls.

I am organized. I am excellent in record keeping.

I get along well with my processor. I bring in only quality loan packages.

I attend the board meeting every week. I am in a good mood. I smile and visit with at least _____ real estate brokers at the meeting.

I have presented to one office each week in _____. I have called the brokers and set the presentation dates by the end of _____.

I have attended two open houses per week. I love to do this. This is a valuable way to spend my time and I have attended at least two open houses per week.

I visit in person with FSBOs. I have visited with at least _____ FSBOs in _____.

I have made the arrangements with at least _____ real estate brokers to qualify all of their buyers by the end of the second week of _____.

I have stopped in at least _____ escrow companies.

I have excellent rapport with brokers and builders. I (state measurable goal with builders).

I have contacted at least _____ new listing agents per week.

I have listed my current offices, target offices by the end of _____.

I have scheduled appointments to meet with the target brokers by the end of the first week of _____. I am a
prospecting machine.

I contact homeowners on a consistent basis.

STOCKBROKERS

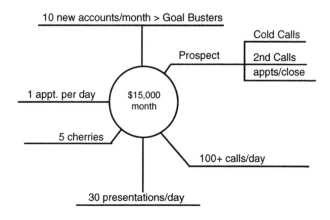

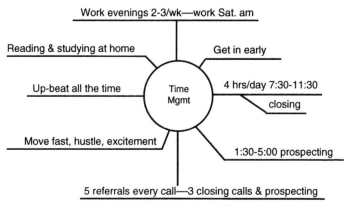

Figure B-5

I am moved, safe, secure, and aroused, as I have grossed at least $_____ in _____. As I love my family, I have grossed at least $_____.

I love to prospect and I do. Prospecting is fun. When I have the phone in my hand I am in an energized state. I feel and am confident, powerful, and strong when I have the phone in my hand. I love cold calls, call-backs, and closing calls.

I make at least 100 dials every day.

I get through to people. I give at least 30 presentations a day. I am confident and persuasive in my presentations. I help people to make the right and profitable choices for the best investments.

I have _____ strong prospective clients per day. I develop _____ strong clients per day.

I have at least one in-person appointment per day.

I ask for the business. I am an expert broker. I know my business and I close. I open at least _____ new accounts this month. I am a goal buster every month.

I love to get up early and I do. I can't wait to get into the office and on the he phone. I get into the office at least by _____ every day.

I sell _____ hours per day. I close. I sell. I closed. I sold.

I prospect from _____ to _____ every day.

I get at least _____ qualified referrals every day. This is my career. I must and I do get at least _____ referrals every day. I get _____ from clients and _____ from prospects.

I am upbeat all the time. As I love (family names), I have a positive attitude all the time. I hustle. I move fast. I am en-thusiastic and moving places. Things are great. I am in a resourceful state all the time.

I read at home. I study. I know all of our products. Because I am knowledgeable, I always handle objections with diversification. I love to study products. I look forward to study at home.

I am focused and dedicated to my career. My purpose in life is to help people have the opportunity for financial growth through investing with me as their financial advisor. Because this is my mission, I gladly work evenings. I work at least _____ evenings per week.

I love to work on Saturday mornings and I worked Saturday mornings every Saturday of _____.

I am consistently in a good mood. I am up and in a good mood all of the time. I was in a good mood all of the time. Always on! Always on!

I am enthusiastic and confident all the time. I am great. I have integrity. This is a good time to invest in the market. This is a good time to invest in the market.

I am self-motivated. I was motivated and energetic every day. I found the wise investments and sold them like my life depended on it. Like my life depends on it, I sell!

I take charge of every call. I am an expert, so I demand in a resourceful and tactful way that people make certain decisions.

I respond to rejection with enthusiasm and positive dollar-producing activity. Rejection is a stepping stone to great accomplishments. I make more phone calls when I get rejected. I made at least 100 dials per day.

People want me to call them and to help them to wisely invest and I do.

I am appreciated and loved. I appreciate and love myself. I am successful. I am a good person. This is a great career and I love it. This is a great career and I love it. This is a great career and I love it. I am great. I am prosperous.

I am organized. I am organized. I plan, the evening before, all of my calls. I am planned and organized.

I diversify. I sold what I should have. I made proper decisions.

I stayed on the phone. I talk to people. I stay on the phone.

I am a competitive fighter. I stick it out. I reached my goals this month. I did what it takes to win and I won. I am successful and focused. I was successful and focused.

PROCRASTINATION

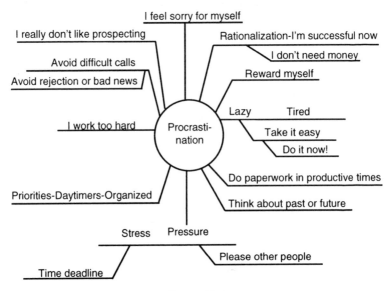

Figure B-6

I am enthusiastic and energetic all the time. I get a great feeling from doing the activities related to the successful accomplishment of my goals. As I love my family, I get a great, loving, caring, secure feeling as I do job-related activities.

I have a do-it-now attitude. I get things done on time or before. I take great pride as I do accomplish a tremendous amount of work in an effective amount of time. I use my time well. Do it now. Do it now. Do it now.

I am flushed, aroused, and excited as I effectively work on a daily basis. I gain strength and energy from my job.

I honor productive and indirectly productive time. I follow

priorities. I do the most productive thing all the time. I do paperwork in non-productive time.

I have a here-and-now attitude all the time. I am focused. I stay in the hear and now. This gives me great energy and focus.

I please myself. I take great pride in the work that I do. I please myself. I am like a scientist in the work that I do and I please myself.

I am at ease and at peace with myself. I like and love myself. I effectively deal with all situations in a positive manner. I have a tremendously positive orientation toward all people and all situations.

I am organized. I am organized. People look to me because I am an example of organization. Because I am organized, I get things done on time or before.

I prioritize my time. I am on time with my Daytimer. I update my Daytimer daily.

I work smart. I gain great joy and satisfaction from my job. My career is my love as well as my hobby. I am serving a great purpose in my life and expressing it through my career. My purpose in life is to _____ and I do.

I love to call difficult clients and I make those calls first. A difficult client means that I have the opportunity to teach that person the value of what I do and I can't wait for that challenge.

I always see rejection as a trigger that moves me to a resourceful state. I respond to rejection with positive, dollar-producing activity. I respond to rejection with enthusiasm and a renewed belief in my product and service and purpose.

I love to prospect and I do. I make _____ calls per day. Prospecting is fun and I love the competitive challenge.

I only have thoughts about myself that forward the action toward the accomplishment of my goals and I do reach my goals every month.

I respond to the challenge of achievement. Although I am already successful, the challenge of achievement keeps me striving every day with a sense of urgency. As I love my family, I strive every day with a sense of urgency.

I reward myself for a job well done. At the beginning of the month, I set up a series of rewards for a job well done. I reward myself for specific activities.

I love to confront myself with result-oriented, measurable, and time-specific activities and I do. I get things done. I am a committed person. I do what I said I would do.

I always listen to my reinforcement "monthly goals" tape every day. The tape helps me focus and accomplish my goals.

TELEMARKETING

I love to cold call, and I do. I am a professional and expert on the phone.

I make people feel at ease on the phone. I relax them and it is a pleasure for people to talk to me on the phone.

I speak with conviction on the phone. I speak with authority. My voice is confident and steady.

As I breathe without effort, I close sales easily.

I focus on the needs of my prospect.

My prospects sense something refreshing about me.

I project positive energy into the minds of my prospects.

I handle objections with ease.

I create rapport from the moment I say, "Hello."

My prospects buy my enthusiasm.

My prospects buy friendship from my voice.

My prospects buy laughter and I give my joy to them freely.

My prospects buy from me because they like me and I am unique.

Secretaries love to put my calls through because they can sense that I bring good news.

I melt ice in people's hearts with my warmth and sincerity.

REAL ESTATE SALES

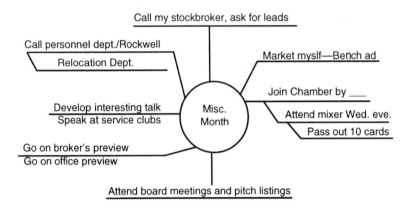

Figure B-7

Door knocking brings results. I knock on ___ doors a day.

I love to knock on doors, and I do.

As I love my family, I knock on ____ doors ____ days per week. Knocking on doors keeps me happy and healthy.

The mail works. I get listings and sales from my mailings. Mailing is worth the time and effort, and I do mail.

I love the phone. I am an expert on the phone.

Every Monday I call the traffic from my open houses. I ask for their business.

I actively talk to _____ FSBOs per week. FSBOs need me. I am great and do list FSBOs.

I take my floor time. I get appointments on floor time. I use my time wisely during floor time.

I love to knock on doors and I do. This is fun. I can't wait to knock on doors.

Homeowners want to hear from me. I see their smiling faces as I talk to them. I hear them thanking me for stopping in. I t feels great to walk my farm.

I am of great service to everyone. I help people.

I quickly get business and referrals from my door knocking.

I have great energy all the time. Knocking on doors energizes me and I do knock on _____ doors per day, _____ days per week.

Knocking on doors brings me happiness, joy, and prosperity. I am happy, joyous, and prosperous.

Appendix C
Sample Weekly Calendar

	Day __ MON	Day __ TUE	Day __ WED	Day __ THU	Day __ FRI	Day __ SAT	Day __ SUN
5 am							
6:00							
7:00							
8:00							
9:00							
10:00							
11:00							
Noon							
1 pm							
2:00							
3:00							
4:00							
5:00							
6:00							
7:00							
8:00							
9:00							

Week of _____

Appendix D
Supplemental Reading

Superlearning. Lynn Shroeder and Sheila Ostrander
Psychic Discoveries Behind the Iron Curtain. Lynn Shroeder
   and Sheila Ostrander
The Roots of Consciousness. Jeffery Mishloue
Using Both Sides of Your Brain. Tony Buzan
Hypnotic Realities. Milton H. Erickson and Ernst Rossi
Human Memory. A.J. Adams
The Psychology of Learning. J.F. Hall
Fitness for Every Body. Linda Garrison and Ann Read
The Brain: A User's Manual. The Diagram Group
Suggestion and Auto-Suggestion. Emile Coue
Doing It Now. Edwin C. Bliss
How to Get Control of Your Time and Your Life. Alan Lakein
"Left Brain/Right Brain". *Saturday Review*, 1975, 2 30-33
Mechanics of the Mind. C. Blakemore
Theories of Learning. E.R. Hilgard and G.H. Bower
Theories of Motivation. R.C. Bolles
*Divided Consciousness: Multiple Controls in Human Thoughts
   and Action.* E.R. Hilgard
Using Your Brain for a Change. Richard Bandler
Sleep: The Gentle Tyrant. W.B. Webb
Beneath the Mask: An Introduction to Theories of Personality.
   C.F. Monte
Change Your Mind and Keep the Change. Steve & Connirae
   Andreas

Doors of Perception. Aldous Huxley
Get the Results You Want. Kostere and Malatesta
Influencing with Integrity. Genie Laborde
Instant Rapport. Michael Brooks
Unlimited Power. Anthony Robbins
Heart of the Mind. Steve and Connirae Andreas

CASSETTE TAPES FOR SUPER ACHIEVEMENT AND PERFORMANCE

BAROQUE MUSIC
Largo Movements
A collection of the slower, 60-beats-per-minute largo movements of baroque music for use in making your reinforcement tape.
1 cassette. **$13.00**

MISSION ACCOMPLISHED
The entire Human Performance Training program recorded in a studio without time constraints and containing all of the available researched and practical information on how to make and use your baroque-music monthly goals tape. If you can't get to the live training program or if you have attended and want to bring the program home in even greater detail, this is the series for you!
8 cassettes and workbook. **$78.00**

HOW TO OVERCOME PROCRASTI-NATION: CONFUSION TO CLARITY
Learn how to overcome procrastination by empowering yourself with the distinctions of time wasted through avoidance of psychological prisons of the "I have to's" and learn the true meaning of FOCUS. Also in this album is Bob Davies at his best in a presentation talking about handling stress with Rational Emotive Style. You will have a reinforcement tape made for you included in this series using the power of baroque music. This will enable you to condition yourself to use the information in this series effortlessly.
3 cassettes and workbook. **$38.00**

THE SUBCONSCIOUS ASPECTS OF PERSUASION
How to appeal to a client's subconscious mind to break their habitual ways of thinking by using precise language. Included is an explanation of personality types and how to sell them. You will also learn of human communication, the creation of rapport, precision probing, and understanding how to sell an idea or product in the way your client likes to buy!
4 cassettes and workbook. **$45.00**

SELF-IMAGE, VISUALIZATIONS AND MIND MAPPING
We have been conditioned to think, feel, and act the way we do. Some of it is good for us and protects us, and some of it is harmful and limits us. Knowledge is Power. • We have become so accustomed to speaking and writing words, we mistakenly assume that normal sentence structure is the best way to remember images and ideas. Now you can learn how to use both sides of your brain to remember information, as well as how to put fun back into learning.
2 cassettes. **$24.00**

LIVING A HEALTHY LIFESTYLE
This series clearly addresses the issue of controlling a habit such as over-eating by exploring the role of food in our lives.You will learn the difference between hunger and appetite. You will experience a TOTAL program with proven results! This series contains new information about diets and breakthrough research on how to make your body an efficient energy-burning machine! 10 cassettes and workbook.
$85.00

SENSORY GOAL SETTING
The human brain has been compared to a hologram by Dr. Carl Pridbram of Stanford. Learn how to neurologically encode high-achievement traits the NLP way.
1 cassette. **$13.00**

CIGARETTE SMOKING
Learn the latest techniques of habit control;. Emphasizes the dangers and addictions of smoking and some outstanding nuts and bolts of how to rid yourself of a controlling habit for good!
1 cassette **$13.00**

ORDER FORM

TITLE	QTY	EACH	SHIPPING WEIGHT	TOTAL
Baroque Music Tape		13.00	2 ounces	
Mission Accomplished		78.00	1 pound	
How to Overcome Procrastination		38.00	1 pound	
Self-Image, Visualization, Mind Mapping		24.00	10 ounces	
Subconscious Aspects of Persuasion		45.00	1 pound	
Living a Healthy Lifestyle		85.00	2 pounds	
Sensory Goal Setting		13.00	2 ounces	
Cigarette Smoking		13.00	2 ounces	
			Subtotal	
			Sales Tax (Calif.)	
			Shipping & Handling	
			Total	

SHIPPING & HANDLING: All orders shipped via ground UPS. Shipping charges: $4 for the first pound + $1 for each additional pound or portion (example: 3 pounds 2 ounces = 4 pounds = $5 shipping)

Payment by: ☐ Check   ☐ Credit Card

(circle one):   Visa   MasterCard   AmEx

Card Number: _____ Exp. Date _____

Name on Card: _____

Signature: _____

Name _____

Street _____

City _____ Zip _____

State _____

Phone _____
NECESSARY FOR CREDIT CARD ORDERS

PHONE IN OR FAX YOUR CREDIT CARD ORDER FOR SAME-DAY DELIVERY!
Phone 949-223-3704
Fax 949-830-9492

High Performance Training, 20992 Ashley Lane, Lake Forest, CA 92630